Master the Mundane

Master the Mundane

How to Manage Life, Home, and Family as a Mom with ADHD

Amy Marie Hann

Copyright © 2025 by John Wiley & Sons, Inc. All rights reserved, including rights for text and data mining and training of artificial intelligence technologies or similar technologies.

Published by John Wiley & Sons, Inc., Hoboken, New Jersey.
Published simultaneously in Canada.

ISBNs: 9781394308149 (Hardback), 9781394308163 (ePDF), 9781394308156 (epub).

No part of this publication may be reproduced, stored in a retrieval system, or transmitted in any form or by any means, electronic, mechanical, photocopying, recording, scanning, or otherwise, except as permitted under Section 107 or 108 of the 1976 United States Copyright Act, without either the prior written permission of the Publisher, or authorization through payment of the appropriate per-copy fee to the Copyright Clearance Center, Inc., 222 Rosewood Drive, Danvers, MA 01923, (978) 750-8400, fax (978) 750-4470, or on the web at www.copyright.com. Requests to the Publisher for permission should be addressed to the Permissions Department, John Wiley & Sons, Inc., 111 River Street, Hoboken, NJ 07030, (201) 748-6011, fax (201) 748-6008, or online at http://www.wiley.com/go/permission.

The manufacturer's authorized representative according to the EU General Product Safety Regulation is Wiley-VCH GmbH, Boschstr. 12, 69469 Weinheim, Germany, e-mail: Product_Safety@wiley.com.

Trademarks: Wiley and the Wiley logo are trademarks or registered trademarks of John Wiley & Sons, Inc. and/or its affiliates in the United States and other countries and may not be used without written permission. All other trademarks are the property of their respective owners. John Wiley & Sons, Inc. is not associated with any product or vendor mentioned in this book.

Limit of Liability/Disclaimer of Warranty: While the publisher and author have used their best efforts in preparing this book, they make no representations or warranties with respect to the accuracy or completeness of the contents of this book and specifically disclaim any implied warranties of merchantability or fitness for a particular purpose. No warranty may be created or extended by sales representatives or written sales materials. The advice and strategies contained herein may not be suitable for your situation. You should consult with a professional where appropriate. Further, readers should be aware that websites listed in this work may have changed or disappeared between when this work was written and when it is read. Neither the publisher nor authors shall be liable for any loss of profit or any other commercial damages, including but not limited to special, incidental, consequential, or other damages.

For general information on our other products and services or for technical support, please contact our Customer Care Department within the United States at (800) 762-2974, outside the United States at (317) 572-3993 or fax (317) 572-4002.

Wiley also publishes its books in a variety of electronic formats. Some content that appears in print may not be available in electronic formats. For more information about Wiley products, visit our web site at www.wiley.com.

Library of Congress Control Number: 2025020911 (Print)

Cover Design: Wiley
Cover Images: © Jane Kelly/stock.adobe.com
Author Photo: © The Branded Boss Lady Photography

SKY10122681_072325

*To my children,
who are my greatest
inspiration and motivation.*

Contents

Introduction		ix
Chapter 1	Understanding ADHD	1
Chapter 2	How ADHD Impacts Motherhood	17
Chapter 3	Master Your Days	31
Chapter 4	Master the Fundamentals	47
Chapter 5	Master Your Daily Rhythm	73
Chapter 6	Master Your Weeks	81
Chapter 7	Master Your Months	93
Chapter 8	Master the Extras	105
Chapter 9	Master Your Emotions	115
Chapter 10	Master Your Energy	129
Chapter 11	Automate Your Life	147
Chapter 12	Troubleshooting	159
Chapter 13	Pulling It All Together	181

Contents

Supporting Resources	187
Sources	189
Acknowledgments	193
About the Author	195
Index	197

Introduction

Dear Reader,

Let's pretend that you are sitting right here with me at this random table at my hometown Starbucks, shall we?

I don't know about you, but I don't get enough of that in this season of life, and there is something deeply restorative about sitting face to face with someone who really gets me. And as a 40-something mom with ADHD, raising three kids with ADHD, I don't get to do that with too many people on the regular.

My greatest hope in writing this book is that you'd walk away with that restorative, "I feel seen and understood" feeling.

Yes, I'm going to share lots of practical tips and insights because I know that you crave actionable steps to make your daily life a little easier, so trust me when I say that lots of those are coming.

But as I share my own self-discovery journey, I hope to empower you to better understand your brain, your needs, and your desires for your life and family. I hope you go from "me too!" to "Wow, I never thought about it that way!"

And as I believe that every great conversation starts with the essential step of history-giving, I'm going to start by sharing a little bit of my personal journal in learning to thrive in motherhood with ADHD.

You see, I'm a little bit of an ADHD unicorn in that I was diagnosed in kindergarten in the mid-'80s with ADD (as it was then called). I consider myself extremely fortunate to have had the support of medicine most of my life, though my understanding of the implications was very limited. It's kind of a miracle that I was even diagnosed, but the science and understanding of things like behavior modification or emotional regulation just weren't around back then.

Throughout my school years, my understanding was that ADHD was a school/success problem and it didn't really impact other areas of my life. If I took my medicine, I did well in school, and that was addressed. And because I did well in school, I thought my ADHD was under control.

Looking back now, I can see how my ADHD impacted so many areas of my life—my self-confidence, my emotions, and my relationships. I also believe that I did well in school because I liked school and was highly motivated by getting good grades. I know now that managing ADHD is a lot more involved.

In my early 20s, life got a lot more complicated, and my ADHD struggles became more transparent, but that core belief remained the same. I thought ADHD was a school and work focus problem. And though school hadn't been challenging for me, work was a different story.

My life felt like a constant roller coaster of taking on too much until I'd burn out and then believe that I was capable of less and take a boring, easy job below my capabilities. Once I got stir-crazy from the tedium, I'd then take some new challenging, exciting position with very little life balance. And the up-and-down roller coaster continued.

I needed challenge and stimulation and was smart and capable, yet I couldn't figure out how to get the right amount of challenge without overextending myself.

After I got married, I began biding my time until I could be a stay-at-home mom. I basically assumed that the whole roller coaster problem would go away once I became a mom. I have always loved kids and been very energetic, so I assumed that motherhood would be where I'd really shine.

Flash-forward five years to 30-year-old me as a stay-at-home mom of my first child and it took me only three months to realize just how wrong I'd been. I mistakenly thought that once I walked away from my corporate job, I'd have more energy for the monotonous home tasks like cleaning and organizing and exercise, but my struggles were only magnified by the lack of structure, routine, and solitude.

Introduction

I had finally arrived at this season of life that I'd longed for and yet it was so much harder than I ever imagined. In fact, it was much harder than being a young professional or student. It was deeply discouraging and hard to share those struggles with others. I felt so much shame about my struggles, especially because I'd wanted to be a stay-at-home mom so badly and had given up any ambitions of a successful career.

I found that I truly didn't enjoy (and even hated) so many things about motherhood that I thought I'd love: planning class parties, volunteering for field trips, going to the playground—it all was so dull and yet also overstimulating.

Don't get me wrong; I was still doing all those boring things. If you asked someone in my life back then, they'd probably tell you that I was supermom. I was *way* overcompensating by overextending myself and trying to live up to the Pinterest-perfect idea of motherhood in order to mask my internal struggles. I was still on the burnout roller coaster, taking on too much out of boredom, only to then get totally overwhelmed. I might have looked like I had it all together, but inwardly I was frustrated, restless, exhausted, and lonely. Behind closed doors I was coping with those feelings in unhealthy ways that left me feeling humiliated.

And as I had more kids, it all just got harder and more discouraging. Finally, I hit a massive wall after having my third child and starting perimenopause.

I was still on medicine. I was in therapy. I was exercising consistently. And yet I was floundering under the mental load of managing my daily life. I was trying so hard and yet I felt like I was drowning in dishes, cleaning, and laundry. And the massive amount of shame and insecurity didn't do anything for my self-esteem or self-confidence.

Meanwhile, all three of my kids (Bowman, Frank, and Libby) as well as my husband (Mark) were also diagnosed with ADHD, and we also have a fair bit of autism spectrum disorder in the mix to keep things interesting.

As I began to learn about ways to help them, I realized that though I'd been diagnosed with ADD as a child, there were so many implications that I hadn't unpacked. I realized that even though I knew I have ADHD, I'd spent most of my life trying to fit in with the world around me. When I couldn't, I just assumed that meant I was capable of less and lowered my bar or my goals.

I didn't realize that my ADHD has massive implications for every area of my life and that it was unrealistic to expect myself to follow the same instruction manual as my neurotypical mom friends raising neurotypical kids. Doing so was making me feel like a failure and adding to the overwhelm and discouragement.

It wasn't just managing the boring daily tasks of life like laundry, dishes, cleaning, and meals, though that was part of it.

It wasn't just managing my own mental health struggles and finding time for exercise and sleep while being a mom of young kids, though that was part of it.

It wasn't just learning how to accommodate the needs of multiple neurodivergent kids with big needs that often seemed to conflict, though that was part of it.

It wasn't just managing the ADHD roller coaster of taking on too much and then burning out, though that was part of it.

It wasn't just how to get myself and my kids the stimulation that we desperately need without me or them getting overstimulated, though that was part of it.

It wasn't just managing my time and my energy, though that was part of it.

It wasn't just learning to regulate my emotions so that I didn't become a rage monster daily with my kids, though that was part of it.

It wasn't just learning to make time for my big ideas and creative interests, though that was part of it.

> *It was all of it. How in the world could I create a life that addressed all these big needs without sinking in to complete despair?*

It was all of it. How in the world could I create a life that addressed all these big needs without sinking in to complete despair?

I was already diagnosed with ADHD. I was already on ADHD medicine. I had read so many books on ADHD and been in therapy for years. And yet I was still massively struggling.

And since no one was talking about *all* these things and there was no instruction manual to follow, I realized I would have to create my own. I began to read every resource that I could get my hands on and gave myself permission to think outside the box around how I manage my home, my time, my energy, and my family in relation to what I was learning about my brain.

I began to take seriously my need for stimulation and challenge and gave myself permission for my days to look different than those of the women around me.

I began to own my challenges and to find work-arounds for me and my family so that my ADHD wouldn't be an excuse or a hindrance to having a happy, healthy, thriving family life.

I began to prioritize self-care and the big needs of my children and let go of many of the "shoulds" that plagued me for so many years.

I began to believe that my creative brain has value to bring to the world and to confidently own my big goals and big ideas and take steps to bring them to life.

I began to own my ADHD quirks and stopped wasting my energy trying to fit into a mold that had never worked for me.

I began to slowly mourn the visions I had for motherhood and began to embrace and even *(gasp!)* love the family life that my husband and I have created.

I began to step in to my big gifts and stopped playing small, knowing that my ADHD brain is capable of big things.

Slowly, surely, over time I've designed a life as a mom with ADHD that feels really, really good for me and my neurodivergent family.

I've figured out how to stay on top of the boring things in life like laundry, meals, and cleaning, but more importantly, I've figured out how to manage my ADHD, use my gifts in a meaningful way, and support the big needs of my neurodivergent kids.

A few years ago, I turned what I'd learned and implemented in my life into a system that I could teach others. I broke it down step by step so that I could lead others through this same transformation. I have now helped thousands of other moms learn to manage their ADHD and create systems for managing their home life that are realistic and can accommodate the unique needs of their families.

If you're looking for a cleaning schedule and chore chart that you can implement today to transform your life, that's not my specialty. But if you're looking for long-term, lasting change in how you manage your energy, your emotions, your time, your home, and your family, you're in the right place.

This book is designed to be transformative and is intentionally laid out in a specific sequence. I ask you to resist jumping ahead and instead to take your time to work through this book over time. There's no right pace, but each chapter has actionable steps and a fair amount of self-reflection that you'll want to work on before moving to the next chapter.

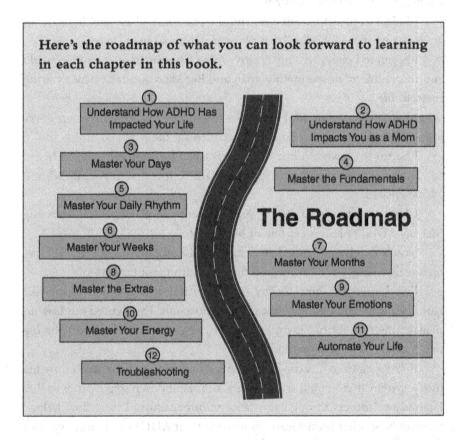

Buckle up and get ready for some major oversharing as I pass along the insights that have transformed my life and family to help you create a life that feels really good to you.

Your Cheerleader,
Amy Marie Hann

1
Understanding ADHD

Before we dig into all the practical tips, it's important to establish a baseline understanding of what ADHD is and how it impacts your daily life. ADHD brains are uniquely wired, and many of the strategies that are most effective in terms of organization and productivity are often very counterintuitive to what you may have heard in the past. It's incredibly important for you to take the time to really understand how your current daily challenges may be connected to your unique ADHD struggles so that you can effectively find solutions to help.

I'm not a physician and I can't diagnose anyone with ADHD. I can, however, provide context and information to help you consider whether to pursue a diagnosis and to help you identify if ADHD-friendly strategies may help you address your biggest struggles.

As I have learned from conversations with thousands of women with ADHD through my online programs and social media following, the most common underlying theme is shame.

If you've spent your life living with undiagnosed ADHD or trying to fit into neurotypical expectations, you probably have a large amount of self-doubt, which unfortunately can get in the way of getting the help and tools that you need. If you assume that your struggles are a result of your own character flaws, you will likely stay stuck assuming that you should be able to fix the problem on your own by trying harder. But if the root problem is ADHD related, you will likely need outside intervention or unique ADHD-friendly strategies to help you create change.

My goal is for this information to be accessible to you and to remove the medical jargon that might make understanding ADHD feel challenging. I want it to be crystal clear about whether a formal ADHD diagnosis and/or ADHD-friendly strategies may benefit you so that you can be empowered and encouraged to get the support you need. And then I'll share the ADHD-friendly strategies that have helped me and others like me manage their home and family life.

10 Things You Need to Know About ADHD

These insights blew my mind and are so important to understand:

1. ADHD is a chronic neurological disorder that impacts professional and academic achievement, relationships, and daily functioning. There are three main presentations of ADHD: inattentive, hyperactive, and combined.
2. ADHD is genetic, so if your kids have ADHD, it is likely present in you or your spouse. If you suspect that you have ADHD, it's likely also present in one or both of your parents.
3. The exact cause of these neurological differences is still unclear, but current research suggests a difference in size and maturity of the prefrontal cortex (PFC) as well as the ineffective transport of dopamine to the PFC. These differences impact how the brain controls attention, emotion, behavior, impulse control, decision-making, and motivation.
4. The PFC may function properly when the ADHD brain is properly activated with the right amount of dopamine and norepinephrine. In other words, when the subject area is new, interesting, or challenging, the PFC might work just fine. When the subject area or task is boring or repetitive, the PFC struggles to function.

5. ADHD symptoms in girls are exacerbated with hormonal changes. Puberty, pregnancy, postpartum, and perimenopause can lead to a spike in ADHD symptoms and an increase in challenges. In women especially, ADHD challenges increase over time. ADHD symptoms are also exacerbated by a woman's monthly cycle and increase at the end/beginning of the menstrual cycle as estrogen levels decrease.
6. ADHD challenges can often get more severe as your challenges in life grow. It might feel like your struggles came out of nowhere but as you better understand ADHD, you will likely see signs of struggle earlier in your life.
7. ADHD in girls is often missed because the diagnostic criteria was created based on hyperactive boys. Many of the inattentive ADHD symptoms are often misinterpreted as character or personality flaws. Many medical practitioners and teachers still aren't well versed in identifying ADHD in girls or women and getting a proper diagnosis for you or your daughter may involve a good amount of self-advocacy.
8. ADHD is often misdiagnosed in women as anxiety. Anxiety is a very frequent biproduct of ADHD struggles, but the root problem is frequently ADHD. You can have both ADHD and anxiety, but it will be hard to lower the anxiety without addressing the ADHD struggles.
9. Emotional dysregulation is a hallmark struggle of those with ADHD. This component of ADHD has come to the forefront of research more recently and was less understood in the past. Emotional dysregulation has major impacts on our daily life and especially on our relationships and ability to parent.
10. ADHD can present very differently in different people. Most people with ADHD have additional comorbidities of some kind, so each of us can have a unique set of challenges.

The Diagnostic Criteria

To get an official ADHD diagnosis as an adult, you need to meet with a trained medical professional (psychiatrist, psychologist, or general practitioner) and they will be looking for you to identify with five of the characteristics shown in the table. They'll also want to hear how these characteristics were present in earlier seasons of your life and in various areas of your life. They may also want to hear about your family of origin and whether ADHD symptoms were present in your parents.

ADHD Diagnostic Criteria, based on the *Diagnostic and Statistical Manual of Mental Disorders, 5th Edition (DSM 5)*

Inattentive Presentation	Hyperactive Presentation	Combined Presentation
Identify with 5 Areas:	*Identify with 5 Areas:*	*Identify with 5 areas from the inattentive presentation list and 5 areas from the hyperactive presentation list.*
• Often fails to pay close attention to details or makes careless mistakes.	• Often fidgets with or taps hands or feet, or squirms in seat.	
• Often has trouble holding attention on tasks or play activities.	• Often leaves seat in situations when remaining seated is expected.	
• Often does not seem to listen when spoken to directly.	• Often runs about or climbs in situations where it is not appropriate.	
• Often does not follow through on instructions and fails to finish projects, chores, or duties in the workplace or at home.	• Often unable to play or take part in leisure activities quietly.	
• Often has trouble organizing tasks and activities.	• Is often "on the go" acting as if "driven by a motor."	
• Often avoids, dislikes, or is reluctant to do tasks that require mental effort over a long period of time.	• Often talks excessively.	
	• Often blurts out an answer before a question has been completed.	
• Often loses things necessary for tasks and activities.	• Often has trouble waiting their turn to speak and frequently interrupts others.	
• Is often easily distracted.		
• Is often forgetful in daily activities.	• Often interrupts or intrudes on others.	

Getting an official diagnosis is a personal decision, but I believe that it can be incredibly validating and can be an important first step in starting your personal ADHD journey. Finding a physician and making an appointment might feel daunting, but I encourage you to take one step at a time.

In working with many moms struggling to get both themselves and their kids support for their ADHD, it's unanimously agreed that it's most helpful to start with yourself. If you first get the help that you need to function, you'll be better able to navigate the steps to help your children.

> **Steps to Getting a Diagnosis**
> 1. Look on your insurance page for psychiatrists in network near you. *Psychology Today* also has a helpful physician search tool.
> 2. Print a list of five options.
> 3. Call or email each office until you find someone who is accepting new patients.
> 4. Once you find a practitioner, make an appointment, even if it feels a long way off. Let go of finding the perfect provider and just start with the easiest appointment you can get. *If you can find an office that allows you to schedule online, jump on that opportunity, because it means you've hit the ADHD jackpot.*
> 5. If you'd like an appointment sooner, keep working down the list.
> 6. Bring your personal notes based on the diagnostic criteria so that you are prepared if the physician asks for examples from your past.

Intensity and Severity

Many of these struggles are present in those without ADHD from time to time. The difference in those with ADHD is in the intensity and severity. It's important to think about the long-term implications of these struggles on an ongoing basis in terms of your career, your finances, your health, and your relationships. These struggles can wreak havoc if left unchecked, unmanaged, and uncontrolled.

> *Everyone is late from time to time. Not everyone gets fired for chronic lateness.*
>
> *Everyone makes an occasional impulsive purchase. Not everyone spends hundreds of dollars on a regular basis on things they don't need.*
>
> *Everyone loses things. Not everyone has to replace phones, wallets, keys, and earphones on a regular basis.*
>
> *Everyone hates doing their taxes. Not everyone has three years of taxes left undone.*
>
> *Everyone interrupts from time to time. Not everyone has limited number of friends because they struggle badly in this area.*

Those might sound like exaggerations, but through my experience I've come to believe that it's universally true that we each have a secret struggle that very few people know about and for which we carry immense shame and guilt. You don't have to identify with all these statements, but spend time thinking about the struggles that impact your daily life the most and consider whether ADHD may be at the root.

If these struggles stay hidden and if you assume, incorrectly, that they are the result of character flaws, change is impossible. You beat yourself up because of these challenges and commit to do better next time. But without treating and accommodating your ADHD, nothing changes.

Many spend an enormous amount of time hiding these struggles or overcompensating in other ways. These challenges are relevant, and when you start looking back at your life and understand your struggles considering your ADHD, a huge weight lifts.

In my experience, here are the additional struggles and manifestations of ADHD that I hear about most commonly that impair and impact daily life and relationships.

Emotional Regulation

Many of us grew up thinking that our emotional responses are part of our personality and we got used to hearing that we are drama queens or too sensitive, but how we respond to our emotions is controlled by our brains and is highly impacted by ADHD. This often looks like having outsized emotions that feel out of our control. We might know that they are irrational and disproportionate to our current reality but feel incapable of reigning them in.

This might look like:

- Having a very short fuse and losing your temper on a regular basis
- Frequent mood swings, which can feel like an emotional roller coaster for your loved ones
- Low frustration tolerance where you get easily derailed by small inconveniences of life
- Strained familial relationships and frequent broken friendships
- Frequent negative self-talk and beating yourself up
- Deeply impacted by the moods of others
- Addictive tendencies as a means of coping with these intense feelings

My emotional regulation struggles presented mostly in ongoing struggles with overeating and overdrinking for most of my life. I am a deeply feeling sensitive soul and feel strongly for the people I love the most. I didn't learn how to process and express my intense emotions in healthy ways, so I buried them to cope and to fit in with the world around me.

For many years, I thought that I was managing my ADHD well but at the same time I was secretly binge-eating and drinking too much. I had shame and regret about those choices, but it took me a long time to realize that they were connected to my ADHD. I'm not alone in this struggle, and research shows that those with ADHD are significantly more likely to develop addictions to food, alcohol, and drugs.

As I began to get more curious about my alcohol consumption, I read many books about addiction and though I knew that I needed help breaking this habit, I didn't identify with much of the recovery language. It didn't feel like it was really getting to the root of why I was so prone to turn to alcohol, especially in social situations. And sadly, using alcohol as a tool for coping with ADHD only made life harder. It increased my anxiety, made my brain foggier, and made it hard to get restorative sleep.

When I dug into the ADHD literature, it became clear that my overconsumption was really rooted in my ADHD. As I got better at managing my ADHD and my emotions, abstaining became much easier.

Executive Function Challenges

The PFC plays a key role in the brain's ability to perform and execute executive functioning. Those with ADHD have a lower capability and capacity around executive functioning. That sounds incredibly grim, but once you understand this problem, these executive functioning challenges can be addressed with ADHD-friendly strategies.

What Are the Executive Functioning Skills and How Do They Impact Your Daily Life?		
Skill	**What**	**Example**
Planning	Making and setting realistic goals and knowing the steps needed to be taken.	Consistently overextend or overcommit your time and energy, which prevents you from meeting goals.
Time management	Knowing how long things take and planning accordingly.	Struggle setting realistic timelines and goals. Often late and frequently double-book yourself.
Working memory	Being able to recall new information quickly.	Struggle recalling words and basic information. Struggle thinking quickly on your feet.
Task initiation	The ability to start and finish tasks without outside accountability.	Know what you should do but struggle taking the steps to get started.
Prioritizing	Knowing what is important and being able to prioritize accordingly.	Everything feels important, which makes it hard to start anything. This can often feel paralyzing.

Flexibility	The ability to adapt to changes.	Hard to course-correct and adjust when life gets messy.
Decision-making	Having clarity in making decisions.	Frequently paralyzed when given too many options.
Organization	The ability to create and use systems for keeping track of things and information.	Struggle managing details like email, physical mail, and texts. Frequently miss details or lose important information.
Motivation	The ability to make yourself do things without outside accountability or extrinsic rewards.	Struggle to do anything without urgency so frequently wait until the last minute.
Self-monitoring	The ability to observe and correct your own behavior based on the circumstances.	Struggle to speak quietly or have the appropriate tone in interpersonal communication.

The extent to which these struggles impact your daily life can vary from person to person. You might struggle with some of these skills and not with others. Your struggles might be more apparent in some contexts (boring, mundane, repetitive) and not as much in your area of interest. This also explains how you might have done well in school but also have ADHD. If you like school and were motivated by good grades, you were able to remember your assignments and do well on tests.

The more executive functioning that your life demands, the greater the extent that you will start to see these challenges impact your daily life. It's not that these challenges weren't there before but likely your lifestyle provided enough margin or bandwidth to accommodate these challenges.

As life gets more complicated (adulthood, career growth, motherhood, more kids, kid's activities, etc.) and your margin for error decreases, these challenges start impacting our daily life in a big way. Living beyond your capacity for an extended period leads to ADHD burnout.

Mental Fatigue and Overstimulation

One of the great misunderstandings about ADHD is around attention. Our brains are exceptional at paying attention to our surroundings but terrible at filtering out unimportant information. The problem lies in our inability to control what gets our attention. This tendency can lead to astute observations and creative insight because we notice things others miss and we often make unique connections, but it can also lead to the common struggle of overstimulation.

Imagine you are going to meet a friend for coffee at your neighborhood coffee shop. This friend happens to have a neurotypical brain that can easily filter out random, unimportant stimuli like background noise or wall art or that conversation happening two tables over or the flickering fluorescent lights, in order to concentrate on you, the person sitting two feet away from her. She can easily recall what you just said five minutes ago and ask an insightful follow-up question. Her brain does these things for her without any intentional effort on her part.

Her brain has a control panel that turns you up to 10 and all the extra stimulation down to 1 because she is there to have coffee with *you*. She is tuned in fully to you and what you have to say. But for your ADHD brain, it is a lot more complicated. Your control panel has every piece of stimuli set to a 10, so everything is fighting equally for your attention. Your brain will be drawn to whatever is most interesting or the loudest.

Even if you want to give your friend your undivided attention, it can be a struggle to do it. Your focus is divided despite your desire to give her your full attention, and it takes an immense amount of mental energy to tune in to what she has to say, not to mention the struggle of recalling information quickly to ask meaningful questions and monitoring your emotions and reactions for appropriateness.

I'm guessing that if you've been living with undiagnosed or misunderstood ADHD, you've lived through many situations just like this one and not thought twice about it. Our brains work harder to do all the normal things of life, and they also absorb a lot more information than our neurotypical counterparts on any given day. That effort and the added stimulation takes a toll, which ends up looking like mental fatigue and overstimulation.

I'm not suggesting that you quit the coffee dates if they are deeply encouraging and rewarding for you. But this sensitivity often leads us to become overstimulated and overwhelmed and we usually don't realize it until it's too late, especially if we aren't intentional about our capacity.

It's not that we are less capable but that these normal situations in life can be more mentally draining for us. This mental fatigue can be unpredictable and hard to explain to others. You and your friend both attend the same one-hour coffee date but, while she may feel energized, you walk away feeling depleted and a little on edge, even though you enjoyed the conversation.

For me, this mental fatigue got so much harder after having kids. Before kids, I had a larger window of time to recover from the daily stimulation of life. After kids, that window became nonexistent because there were always little people talking to me. Motherhood made it very hard to recover from the daily stimulation of life, and this struggle became much more pronounced.

I am guessing that you are nodding along and know exactly what I'm talking about because this mental fatigue and overstimulation are a regular part of your life. You probably know intimately what it feels like to reach this point of overstimulation where you have zero EFs (executive functioning) left to give.

This might look like:

- Feeling incapable of making any decisions
- Feeling overwhelmed and triggered by noise of any kind especially late in the day, which can lead to intense emotions and anger
- Not being able to tolerate touch and needing to be in your comfiest clothes
- Feeling incredibly overwhelmed by visual clutter and toys, which might lead to lots of negative self-talk
- Wanting to hide in your room to avoid your family and responsibilities

ADHD isn't the only reason someone might struggle with overstimulation and mental fatigue, so that alone isn't an indicator that you have ADHD, but it is a major part of living with ADHD and gets exponentially harder after having kids.

Rejection Sensitivity

Many with ADHD identify with a unique condition called rejection sensitivity dysphoria (RSD). It is not a formally recognized symptom or separate diagnosis, but many experts use it in connection with ADHD, especially in women. RSD is a unique emotional regulation struggle specific to any sort of negative emotion or feedback. With RSD, any kind of failure or perceived failure leads to intense and severe emotional pain.

This might look like:

- Feeling severe anxiety before any situation where rejection is a possibility
- Becoming an extreme people pleaser to avoid rejection
- Perceiving any kind of neutral response as negative and a rejection, which can be very self-defeating
- Low self-esteem and easily embarrassed
- Large displays of emotion (rage, anger, crying) with disappointment or rejection
- Struggling to take steps toward goals because of fear of possible rejection
- Social anxiety, which might lead to excessive drinking or eating in social settings to cope with fear of rejection
- Intense feelings leading to social isolation or depression

Perfectionism and Masking

One of the most surprising facts that I found in my research on ADHD is that perfectionism is the most common cognitive distortion reported in adults with ADHD. Considering RSD, this makes a whole lot more sense. If your brain feels immense pain when you perceive any kind of criticism, your brain will work hard to avoid that pain. You will do everything you can to control the narrative around you and to keep up the facade that you make no mistakes.

People assume that a woman with ADHD would appear like a female version of Pigpen from the Charlie Brown comics, with a cloud of dust and chaos following you everywhere you go. And though some women with ADHD might self-identify with words like "messy" or "disorganized," many more appear very organized on the surface. It's their internal lives or even their lives behind closed doors that feel so chaotic and overwhelming.

Almost every woman I talk to with ADHD "feels like a failure" but that doesn't mean that they look like a failure. They may be highly productive, accomplished, well liked, and appear successful to the world around them, but they still feel like they're letting everyone down. They are incredibly hard on themselves, and their cognitive differences make it hard to have realistic expectations of their time and energy.

If I had 10 dollars for every mom with ADHD who has told me that she wants to homeschool multiple children with learning challenges, build a six-figure business, make every meal from scratch, and have a home straight out of HGTV, all without childcare or additional help—I'd be very, very rich. So many women are expecting themselves to have six full-time jobs at once and then beat themselves up for not being able to meet their insane personal expectations.

Others may look at someone with perfectionistic ADHD and think, "There's no way you have ADHD!" because they see the accomplishments, but what they're really seeing is an elaborate mask. They don't see the mental gymnastics performed daily to maintain those excessively unrealistic personal expectations or the accompanying amount of anxiety. This hamster wheel of cognitive struggle and excessive striving is exhausting.

At some point, as the demands of life grow, this hamster wheel becomes no longer feasible, and it can often feel like ADHD came out of nowhere. I call this hitting the ADHD wall, and it can happen at different seasons of life, though for many it comes with motherhood.

This might look like:

- Creating overly complex organization systems to overcompensate for struggles with planning and organization
- Only inviting people over after obsessively cleaning your home to hide disorganization and the struggle to maintain a clean space
- Masking your hyperactivity or social anxiety by overdrinking or overeating in social settings
- Constantly rehearsing conversations and situations to hide any social anxiety, overwhelm, or language processing struggles
- Meticulously following trends in fashion or home decor to hide inner chaos or struggles with executive functioning
- Saying "yes" to everything and overcommitting to mask struggles at home and overcompensate for perceived shortcomings

- Not asking for help from friends or your partner to handle difficulties with managing details and scheduling
- Pretending to enjoy activities and events you don't like to fit in with others, masking sensory sensitivities or unique preferences

Uniquely Gifted

Our brains are wired differently, which comes with complications, but it also comes with many positive attributes. We bring a unique perspective to the world and, because of our ability to consume our environments, we often notice things others miss.

Many of the most creative and innovative thinkers and creators of our time have ADHD. Bill Gates, Greta Gerwig, Mel Robbins, Justin Timberlake, and Richard Branson are among a few of the thought leaders who have shared openly about their own challenges with ADHD. And yet their creative contribution to the world is not *despite* their ADHD challenges but largely *because* of their uniquely wired brains.

I don't think that ADHD is a superpower as some suggest, but I do think that those of us with ADHD have unique gifts that can bring immense good to the world. We have unique areas of immense giftedness where our out-of-the-box thinking, creativity, and curiosity can lead us to great accomplishments.

Common Strengths of Those with ADHD

- **Creativity:** Unique ability to see possibility and create something from nothing.
- **Perseverance:** Relentlessly pursue personal goals and dreams despite setbacks and obstacles.
- **Curious:** Endlessly inquisitive and in pursuit of knowledge and solutions.
- **Intuition:** Excellent instincts and often know and understand things immediately that aren't obvious to others.
- **Adaptability:** Often very good in a crisis and able to change courses quickly and easily.
- **Risk Taking:** The upside to impulsivity is a willingness to take actions and chances that others would fear to pursue.

- **Patterns and Perspective:** Unique perspective and viewpoint on every problem and situation because of our differently wired brains.
- **Innovative:** Have out-of-the-box ideas and find unique solutions to problems.
- **Empathy and Compassion:** Our big emotions often lead us to be very self-aware and highly attuned to the emotions and feelings of others. We often feel what others are feeling.
- **Energy and Enthusiasm:** Often the life of the party and are incredibly fun to be around. Our intensity and enthusiasm can be contagious.
- **Humor:** Unique sense of humor because of our observations of the subtleties of life.
- **People Skills:** Often exceptional at reading people and connecting with people, and an ability to make others feel at ease and to draw them out.
- **Hyperfocus:** Ability to accomplish a great deal in a short amount of time once we find our flow.

I believe that understanding the good in your unique brain is the necessary first step in doing the work of addressing your ADHD struggles. When we believe and embrace that our differently wired brains hold powerful possibility, it frees us to find the solutions and work-arounds we need to live to our fullest potential.

You are allowed to be a complicated, imperfect person who has both amazing gifts and significant challenges. Having ADHD struggles doesn't make your gifts less extraordinary. It just means that you need to learn to accommodate those struggles so that you can live to your fullest potential.

> *You are allowed to be a complicated, imperfect person who has both amazing gifts and significant challenges.*

You aren't broken. You aren't a hot mess. You aren't incapable of change.

You are a creative and curious innovator with so much good to bring the world, your marriage, your home, and your family.

Learning to thrive as a mom with ADHD is just as much about learning to live to your fullest potential in the areas where you shine as it is learning to address the areas where you struggle. You can't address the challenges without also shining light on the good.

Know that as you keep reading this book, I want to bring the hard things to light so that you can find the help that you need, but I also want to help you explore those big ideas that you haven't fully allowed yourself to pursue. I know they're there because it's a fundamental part of what it means to have ADHD. You might not see it yet because you've been so focused on addressing the challenges, but know that I believe it's there. It's waiting for you to believe in yourself and to trust that you are so much more than your ADHD struggles.

Whether you are self-diagnosed or have had a formal evaluation, welcome. You are in good company, and I'm honored to have the opportunity to help you find your rhythm as a mom with ADHD.

> **Exercise: Self Reflection**
> - What does overstimulation and mental fatigue look like for you?
> - Have you hit your ADHD wall? What circumstances led to that for you?
> - What personal challenges from your childhood, teen years, and early adulthood do you now see are connected to ADHD?
> - What ADHD strengths can you identify most clearly in yourself? How do those contribute to your motherhood?

2

How ADHD Impacts Motherhood

I have always loved kids.

As a little girl, I played Barbies and baby dolls for hours on end in my room. I loved playing with younger kids in my neighborhood and babysat as soon as possible and as often as I could. Every job I had in high school and college involved working with kids. Even in my 20s as a young adult and then after I got married, I continued to babysit for several families as a side hustle.

Having kids was never a question for me and always something that I deeply desired to have as part of my life. And yet I was completely unprepared for how much harder motherhood would be for my ADHD brain.

I had a very clear vision of the type of mom that I wanted to be and what I wanted my family to look like:

- *I was going to be the mom who made the cute lunches with a little note inside to make them feel special.*
- *I was going to be present with my kids and play with them for hours on the ground.*
- *I was going to have the put-together family with the latest fashions and trends.*

- *I was going to be class mom and have the type of home where everyone wanted to hang out.*
- *I was going to have the best birthday parties and be the holiday celebration queen.*

I masked my ADHD struggles by looking like I had it all together, so my vision for motherhood was based on looking like I had it all together. I was going to be the perfect mom by looking like the perfect mom. And then I became responsible for keeping another human alive, and that plan kind of crumbled.

The basic tasks of life took far more time and energy than I anticipated. I was struggling with the necessary tasks like cooking, cleaning, laundry, and clutter. And even more importantly, I was struggling with my own self-care basics. How would I get the sleep, exercise, and rest that I needed while also doing all these mundane tasks and keeping this little human alive?

And let's be honest, sometimes managing my mental health feels like a full-time job. One of the reasons I left my corporate role was because I didn't have enough time for exercise or therapy or friends because I know those things help me significantly. But for some reason, it wasn't any easier to make time for those things once I was at home full time with a little person.

But more than anything, my biggest struggle was that it was all so much more boring than I ever imagined. I loved my son, and I had wanted to leave my corporate job to be with him full-time but, man, was I struggling without the mental stimulation of work. And yet I couldn't figure out how to find time for my interests while floundering with the fundamentals.

My vision for motherhood was based on me fitting in with this idealized vision of what a "good mom" looks like. But it didn't take into consideration the needs of my brain or the unique needs of my neurodivergent kids. I felt like a failure because I was trying to force myself to do motherhood in a way that didn't work for my brain or for my family. And in time, I realized that none of the things on my original list aligned with my deepest values.

I had to mourn the vision of my family that I made up in my head and learn to create a vision of motherhood that accounted for the needs of my unique brain and the needs of my neurodivergent family, and that also reflected my values. That started with getting realistic around my capacity for executive functioning and looking at my own personal daily struggles considering my ADHD. I had to stop beating myself up and see that these struggles weren't personality traits or character flaws; they were manifestations of my very real neurological condition.

Motherhood requires an immense amount of executive functioning, and so it only makes sense that as someone who struggles with executive functioning, I'd need to do things differently. As I began to understand how many of my daily struggles were rooted in my executive functioning challenges, and the unique needs of my brain, I began to give myself more compassion and look for solutions.

As I found systems to make the daily tasks of life less draining, I began to have more time and energy for the habits that help me and to pursue my big ideas. I realized that I wasn't a bad mom for needing accommodations. In fact, I now believe that finding accommodations for my challenges makes me an amazing mom. My goals and aspirations for the mom that I want to be are no longer based on just appearing like a perfect mom but instead on modeling for my kids what it looks like to thrive with ADHD.

I began to have hope that if I could better manage my ADHD and find ADHD-friendly strategies for addressing my executive functioning struggles, I could still be a great mom. I wasn't a failure or a hot mess; I just needed to factor in the needs of my unique brain in how I manage my home and family and (even more importantly!) how I design my days.

As I've worked with thousands of moms with ADHD over the years, I've identified a list of common daily struggles that are ADHD related. When you understand that ADHD is at the root of these challenges, you can find work-arounds, systems, and strategies to address them effectively. It also helps to empower you to prioritize the self-care that you need to effectively manage your ADHD.

Common ADHD Struggles in Motherhood

Core Struggle	ADHD Struggle	Might Look Like
Overcommitment	Time blindness and planning	• Frequently double-booking yourself • Like to be busy but take on too much and then drop balls • Chaotic and stressful pace of life that takes a toll on your marriage, family, and health
All or nothing thinking	Perfectionism and planning	• Incredibly productive or a total couch potato • Trouble starting unless it can be perfect • Hard to moderate energy and frequently overdo it and then are exhausted
Time blindness	Time management	• Usually late • Hard to estimate how long things take • Regularly miss appointments and events
Decision paralysis	Task initiation, decision-making, and prioritization	• Get overwhelmed with all that needs to be done and end up doing nothing • Know you need help but get overwhelmed by options • Spend hours researching but fail to take action and have little to show for it
Task completion	Motivation, inattention, task initiation, and planning	• Start new projects but struggle completing them • Get easily distracted and forget what you were doing • Create complicated systems but fail to implement them.
Side quests	Prioritizing and motivation	• Feel like I'm always busy but nothing important gets done • Struggle getting rest and are always tired, though you feel like so much is left undone

Self-doubt	Rumination, perfectionism, decision-making, and RSD (rejection sensitivity dysphoria)	• Spend a lot of time doubting decisions or worrying about past decisions • Frequently second-guess decisions or systems you've created • Don't trust your ideas enough to implement them • Spend a lot of time in "creation" mode but fail to follow through with anything
Procrastination	Planning, time management, and motivation	• Do everything last minute, which leads to excessive ongoing stress • Know what you should do earlier but can't make yourself act without urgency
Loneliness and lack of support	Impulsivity, anxiety, planning, perfectionism, and RSD	• Lack close friends though you want connection and need support • Don't invite anyone over because of fear of rejection and shame of the chaos • Don't feel known by others after years of masking and perfectionism
Easily distracted	Attention, overstimulation, planning, and motivation	• Easily distracted in the middle of each task and then struggle to finish what you are doing • Hard to get anything done with kids in the home • Easily distracted and overwhelmed by the sounds of your busy kids
Lack of boundaries	Perfectionism and people pleasing	• Say yes to things you don't enjoy, don't want to do, or aren't able to do • Delay basic self-care because of putting the needs of others before taking care of yourself
Lack of margin	Planning, organization, and time management	• Chaotic pace of daily life with no room for life interruptions (sick kids, job loss, death, etc.) • Very anxious, waiting for the other shoe to drop • Can't ever get ahead because of the roller coaster of drama

Okay, let's pause here. The point of this chart isn't to make you feel like a complete mess. I want you to look at the chart and star the two core challenges that are most impacting your daily life. As you go through this book, keep those two areas front of mind. Give yourself permission to focus on those initially. No matter how many of these struggles you identify with, I want you to know that you aren't alone! And you aren't broken. You aren't incapable of change and growth. You have a uniquely wired brain, and addressing your core struggles requires understanding your unique capacity, your unique needs, and your children's unique needs.

You have a uniquely wired brain, and addressing your core struggles requires understanding your unique capacity, your unique needs, and your children's unique needs.

Executive Functioning Capacity

We aren't incapable of doing boring things that require executive functioning, but we are limited in our capacity. This is why, looking back, it seems like I had a handle on managing my life, but as I had more kids, my abilities tanked. More people required more executive functioning, and my life was then requiring more than I had to give on a regular basis.

It helps me to think about EF (executive functioning) as a unit of measurement. Before kids, I had enough EF to do the basic things of life. But as I had more kids, built a business, and life in general got more complicated, my life required more EF than I had to give.

The result was that my daily life was running on a daily EF deficit. I was going further and further into the red each day, until I eventually hit burnout.

Imagine going over your budget each month to find yourself in massive debt over time. Living beyond your means catches up to you and the result isn't pretty. The same is true if you are living outside of your mental energy capacity.

Thriving in motherhood with ADHD requires learning to understand your capacity and learning to live within your means.

Thriving with ADHD requires learning to understand your capacity and learning to live within your means. When you know and accept your personal capacity, you can then plan your life accordingly.

This level of self-awareness in time makes it much easier to live within your capacity and avoid burnout.

Need for Challenge

ADHD brains thrive on novelty, challenge, and interest. Understanding and embracing this is so important, but our need for challenge can also get complicated.

If our lives are too dull and boring, we will struggle more with the mundane daily things of life. I think of this as the boredom zone. When we are bored, it's like our brains struggle to function. We have even less EF than normal. We tend to struggle with unhealthy coping mechanism like procrastination here too. And we often turn to unhealthy habits like doomscrolling, online shopping, sugar, or alcohol to numb the feeling of boredom and get some stimulation.

As I look back on my life, I can see this trend so clearly. Some of the hardest years were the ones where I was bored and mentally understimulated. That boredom frequently led me to unhealthy habits and self-sabotage, which made it even harder to do the boring tasks of daily life:

- Switching to an easier major in college, only for it to be too easy
- That first real job that had great work-life balance where I spent most of the day twiddling my thumbs
- That job with a small organization where I was expected to be a receptionist waiting for menial tasks that was deeply unfulfilling

Boredom has always been my kryptonite, but it took me becoming a mom to get it.

Looking back on my early motherhood years, this need became even more glaring. I planned my first child's baptism before he was even born. If you'd have asked me then, I probably would have given you some grand reason why I needed to spend the first seven weeks of his life planning and hosting an elaborate Mother's Day brunch for 50 people, but I see now that I was just bored and needed a new project.

At the time, we lived in small rental house in the Washington, DC, area with a huge yard. Hosting this brunch meant that I was signing up my husband (also a brand-new parent!) to extensively clean up this huge backyard for the brunch. He and my dad spent an exhausting weekend completely overhauling the overgrown landscaping while my mom and I cooked an elaborate spread for my nearest and dearest. It was beautiful and special but also unnecessarily stressful and exhausting for me, my husband, and my parents.

I look back now and wonder, "What was I thinking?!" but the truth is that I wasn't thinking. When I'm not intentionally challenged and getting the mental stimulation my brain needs, my mind tends to go rogue. I become fixated on random projects, which then become urgent needs, whether or not I have the time, energy, or money to complete them. I could write a list a mile long of the random side projects/obsessions that have captivated me over the years, and I'm guessing that you can too.

Explaining the boredom zone to those who aren't wired this way can be challenging. They might see your struggles to stay on top of the boring tasks of life and assume that you shouldn't add more to your plate until you can get a handle on those tasks, not understanding that your brain needs a certain amount of challenge to function. Only you know your unique need and your personal capacity for challenge. You must learn to advocate for yourself and find a right-sized challenge for your life.

Looking back at the baptism brunch example, in hindsight I can see that probably wasn't the right-sized challenge for that season of my life. It was a very stressful few weeks and not the best use of my very short maternity leave. I don't regret having my son baptized but I should have waited a little longer and not added that pressure to myself as a brand-new mom. I would have been better served to find a small hobby to do in that unique season, knowing that I needed a project other than a massive event.

It's essential that we have outlets for mental challenge and for stimulation, but we must find that in a way that works for our capacity. Just as boredom is unhealthy for us, so is overcommitment and unfortunately our brains tend to want to say yes to every new challenge that comes our way. We love challenge and novelty, so this tendency makes complete sense, but we must know our own limits.

If we take on too much challenge, we will venture into the depletion zone. There are unique challenges in both the boredom zone and the depletion zone. And I can tell you that I've been in both over the years.

Depletion Zone
Overcommitted, Overextended + Overstimulated
Living outside EF capacity
On Road to ADHD Burnout
MARGIN
Activation Zone
Intentionally Managing the Mundane Things of Life
Managing ADHD Through Self-Care + Stimulation
Healthy Mix of Challenge, Interest + Novelty
Operating with in Your EF Capacity
Optimal Creativity + Clarity
Boredom Zone
Understimulated because life is boring + mundane
Struggle with task initiation and paralysis
Struggle with procrastination because relying on urgency to meet any demands.
High Stress + High Insecurity

The depletion zone is when our life requires more executive functioning than we have. This happens from time to time due to circumstances outside our control like moving, job loss, sickness, or especially hard seasons of life. Unfortunately, due to our need for challenge, we very often get into the depletion zone because of our own choices. You know, like planning a brunch for 50 people while having a brand-new baby.

This might look like:

- Having unrealistic expectations around our executive functioning capacity
- Having unrealistic expectations of our time and energy based on our current capacity
- Taking on new commitments out of boredom, only to end up taking on too much
- Not taking into consideration the big needs of our neurodivergent kids
- Neglecting the mundane things of life out of boredom until they pile up

This often happens because of having very little margin in our lives. ADHD brains love urgency, and we can rely heavily on it to get things done in life. When a deadline is quickly approaching, we can motivate to get things done because of the adrenaline rush. This often works well in our teens and 20s, but urgency isn't a great strategy for doing the mundane things of life. Urgency is effective but it's also stressful. And that stress adds up over time.

When I was 23 and got off work at 5 p.m. and had no plans for dinner and no groceries in the house, I could run by Trader Joe's and pick up whatever I was craving and come home and cook it up. It wasn't ideal and I probably wasted money, but I could still be sitting down to eat by 7 p.m. At 31, when I'd get off work at 5:30 p.m., then pick up my son from daycare and realize that I had no idea what was for dinner, it looked a lot different. Running into the store with a cranky toddler takes a *lot* more executive functioning and is a recipe for overwhelm and overstimulation.

Relying on urgency as a daily motivator to enable you to do the small things of daily life no longer works like it once did. The daily stress of it takes a toll and adulting is stressful enough. You must save your margin for the normal stressful things of life outside of your control, like job loss, moving, sickness, or death, that are normal to the human experience. If you go into the depletion zone daily because of small mundane tasks like deciding what's for dinner, life will be exhausting and overwhelming.

In contrast, the activation zone is where we learn to live within our capacity while also making time for the stimulation and challenge, we need to thrive. Learning to find the right amount of challenge and living within your capacity is essential to thriving in motherhood with ADHD. The steps of this book are intentionally laid out to help you create a life in the activation zone.

ADHD Burnout

ADHD burnout is when you reach a state of mental, physical, and emotional exhaustion. It happens when you've been living outside your means in the depletion zone for an extended period. Most women I work with don't even realize that they have ADHD until they hit burnout. As they try and navigate their mental health and get to the root of their struggles, they discover ADHD. Burnout is feeling like your EF bank is completely overdrawn and you have no more EFs left to give.

This might look like:

- You feel stuck in unhealthy coping habits that are bringing a lot of shame.
- Daily life feels very chaotic and you don't even know where to start to create change.

- You feel very disconnected from what you enjoy.
- You struggle to fall and stay asleep but are always tired.
- Brain fog and executive functioning challenges make daily life incredibly challenging.
- It feels impossible to make one more decision even if it's incredibly small.

I knew that I had ADHD but still managed to hit ADHD burnout because my personal expectations were so out of whack with the needs of my brain. I was expecting my life to look like the neurotypical moms raising neurotypical kids around me and didn't understand that my life would look very, very different. I was spending so much time trying to fit in and I had to learn to make space for the unique needs of my brain.

Your Unique Needs

When I say that I wasn't prepared for the immense challenges that my ADHD would present for motherhood, what I really mean is that I didn't think that ADHD would impact how I needed to live. I didn't think I'd need a different instruction manual for how I design my days, parent my kids, or care for my home.

When I first left my corporate job to stay home with my then-18-month-old son, it was a tough transition for me. I remember telling another mom how I'd been staying up until one in the morning reading because my brain was bored and needed something to toil on after a day spent with a toddler. She looked at me like I was a crazy person. She absolutely didn't relate to my need for mental stimulation. Sure, she didn't like doing the dishes or cooking meals, but she didn't need mental stimulation in the same way that I did.

For years I felt so alone and weird because I had this insatiable need for mental stimulation and challenge that other moms around me didn't have. And though I was trying to make time for my business ideas, I still felt the need to show up in other areas of life as they did. I felt the need to mask my differences and appear as "normal" as possible.

When I realized that I couldn't keep up with the other moms around me, I felt like a huge failure. And as I talked to other moms like me, I learned that feeling is pretty much universal. So many women feel like a failure because they can't do life in the same way as the neurotypical moms around them. If you experience similar feelings, you aren't alone.

But I am not a failure, and neither are you. Our differently wired brains have unique needs that must be factored in to how we spend our time and energy. It's unrealistic to compare ourselves to women who don't have these same needs.

This might look like:

- The need for mental stimulation like work outside of the home, hobbies, and projects
- The need for vigorous exercise because of physical hyperactivity and difficulty sitting still or sleeping
- The need for frequent downtime to recover from social gatherings because you are easily overstimulated
- The need for structure and routine and the struggle with a change in plans or spontaneity
- The need for spontaneity and fun and a struggle with monotony
- The need for a break from your kids to think clearly and get anything done

ADHD can look a lot of ways, and your needs may differ from mine, but they are still valid and important. Self-awareness and self-acceptance are necessary steps in this process. You must own up to your needs before you can start making them a priority. Designing a lifestyle where you prioritize your essential needs, understanding that your days will likely look different from others you know, is incredibly important.

Raising Neurodivergent Kids

Raising kids with ADHD is by far the hardest thing I've ever done but it's also been the biggest motivator for me. My personal growth journey skyrocketed after my oldest son was diagnosed. Understanding my own ADHD brain enabled me to better understand and help him.

Raising children is hard for all parents, but children with ADHD have unique needs, and parenting them well is often counterintuitive to traditional parenting methods. These efforts take mental and emotional energy as well as our time.

This might look like:

- Kids struggle with self-monitoring, making them very loud and they often talk nonstop, which can be overstimulating.
- Kids may have a lot of energy and need extra time playing outside.
- There may be cognitive differences requiring tutoring or therapy.
- Navigating doctors' appointments and medicine refills.
- Accommodating picky eaters and sensory needs.
- Dealing with behavior challenges.

Factoring in these needs affects how you design your days and establish your personal expectations. I've read countless books about parenting ADHD children, and it always seems like they're talking to someone in a vacuum, as if parenting kids with ADHD is the only demand on your plate. Their needs must be taken into consideration, but they have to be part of the bigger picture of your life.

The Solution

For years, managing my life as a mom with ADHD felt like one never-ending mind game. I love a good problem to solve and I hate to lose, so I kept trying different strategies and tactics, attempting to figure out how to make all the pieces fit. I was trying to be a great mom, take care of my home, manage my mental health, pursue my big ideas, and help my kids care for their big needs.

I was still trying to fit in with the moms around me and look like I had it all together. The solution came when I finally admitted to myself that the pieces were just never going to fit. At first that realization was defeating, but in time I've come to see that it's liberating.

> I realized that . . .
>
> *My brain is wired differently and has unique needs.*
> *My kids are wired differently, and they have unique needs.*

> *My days will look differently because of these unique needs.*
> *My life will look differently because of these unique needs.*
>
> *I can do life differently and still be a great mom.*
> *I can do life differently and still have a great life.*
> *I can do life differently and create a beautiful family culture for my children.*

When I realized these things, everything changed.

I finally had the permission that I needed to find solutions that worked for me and family and design my life in a way that worked for me and the actual people in my family. I stopped wasting my energy masking my ADHD struggles and trying to blend in with the moms around me. Instead, I gave myself permission to create a system that worked for me and my brain and to ignore what everyone else was doing. Once I let go of my preconceived visions of what it looks like to be a good mom, I came to see that reality can be so much better.

> *Being a great mom with ADHD means designing my life in a way that works for me, my brain, and the unique needs of my neurodivergent family. My life will look different from others and only I can do this work.*

Exercise: Self-Reflection

- Which two of the common struggles listed on page 20 are having the biggest impact on your daily life in this current season of life?
- Can you identify a specific season of your life where you were in the boredom zone?
- Can you identify a specific season of your life where you were in the depletion zone?
- What unique needs do you have because of your ADHD?
- What unique needs do your children have because of their neurodivergence?

3
Master Your Days

As for so many, 2020 was the hardest year of my life but it really started for me way before the pandemic started. 2019 was a huge doozy for me.

My first son was born in 2011 and when I became a stay-at-home mom in 2012, the plan was for us to have a second child shortly thereafter. Well, that didn't happen. After trying everything short of IVF, we experienced eight years of secondary infertility. I became pregnant with my daughter miraculously with no intervention in March of 2018.

In those years of waiting, we became foster parents and had the privilege of welcoming several children into our home, including one sweet two-year-old boy we'd later have the privilege of adopting. Shortly after our daughter was born, after two years of fostering Frank, we went to trial. Nine months later, in September of 2019, his adoption was finalized.

Foster care is a beautiful thing and there is a huge need. It is also incredibly stressful and after the adoption went through, I realized that I'd been holding my breath for two and half years, not knowing what would happen to this sweet boy who had captured my heart so fully. Though I was incredibly thankful and grateful, I was also emotionally exhausted from those years of hoping and longing.

Two months after Frank's adoption, two huge things happened to our family.

In November 2019, my father-in-law (then 87) became ill and was then in the hospital for a month. He came home in December 2019 and was in our home on hospice care through September 2020, when he passed away. My mother-in-law was his full-time caregiver, and there were medical workers in and out of the house daily. Their small living area in our home became a hospital room. There were many close calls, and it was emotionally exhausting for everyone in our home.

While he was in the hospital initially and we were expecting him to come home and recover, we got a phone call about an additional foster care placement. There was a little girl who needed a home. We had a bed for her, and it was right before Christmas, and I said yes because I didn't have any reason to say no.

I was barely hanging on by a thread. This child needed so much more help than I could give, and there were very problematic behavior challenges. Her anger triggered me, my husband, my mother-in-law, and my kids. At the time, I didn't know how to regulate my emotions, and my main coping mechanism was to hide in my room and then to drink wine to numb the overwhelm as soon as I could get away with it.

This is what my daily life looked like *before* the pandemic hit. All three bigger kids were in school, so I had a brief respite during the day while the baby napped. When that was ripped away in March 2020 and I was responsible for educating these three kids and navigating the emotional regulation and behavior challenges all day long, I completely fell apart.

I was totally burned out and living so far past my capacity that the small tasks of daily life felt impossible, and I just wanted to hide in my room.

I was yelling a lot.

I was drinking a lot.

I was overstimulated all the time.

I felt like a failure in pretty much every area of my life.

Ongoing Capacity Struggles

I can look back now and say, "Wow, you were trying to do way too much," but in the moment it all felt necessary because I had no way to gauge my capacity. My brain loves challenge and novelty, so each new thing felt like something to conquer, and I didn't feel like any one new thing was too much until I was absolutely drowning.

Over time, I've come to accept a few hard truths about my ADHD brain that informed how I created my system and ultimately led to me learning how to live long term in the activation zone. Instead of hoping or wishing that these things would change, I chose to plan for them and committed to finding a strategy for managing my life considering these truths.

> **Hard Truths About My ADHD Brain**
>
> - My curious and creative brain will *always* want to do more than is humanly possible. I must create constraints and boundaries around my capacity to stay out of the depletion zone.
> - My brain really hates doing boring, monotonous tasks. Beating myself up about this isn't helpful. Instead, I need to shift my focus to being *proud* of all the boring things I do because ADHD brains thrive on positive reinforcement.
> - I can do boring things and tasks that require executive functioning but I am limited in my capacity. I must be intentional and strategic around my EF capacity as I create expectations for myself. I must identify and prioritize what matters the most to me and my family in my current season of life.
> - Making plans and prioritizing demands burns through my limited executive functioning capacity. I need a clear, realistic plan for my ongoing demands that doesn't require me to make daily decisions. A clear plan that I can follow means more mental energy each day.
> - No matter how much time and intentionality I commit to creating a plan, I will forget about it. I need clear visuals and automation to make the plan easy for me to remember and follow.
> - I must be fully invested in the creation of the system for it to stick. It has to be personalized to the needs of me and my family but I also need to have autonomy in how I implement and live out this system.
>
> *(continued)*

> (*continued*)
> - My energy is inconsistent and any plan that requires me to have the same energy every day is doomed to fail. I need flexibility and permission to do less on some days.
> - My brain tends to want to change every area of my life at once. I like to create big, complicated systems but this never works out long term. Actual change happens when I give myself permission to focus on a few areas at a time. This also requires intentionally putting problem areas on the back burner while I focus on the most urgent needs.
> - It's extremely hard for me to think clearly when I'm in mom mode. I don't make good decisions about my capacity on the spot or in the moment. I need a system for my EF capacity that helps me to preplan as much as possible to limit this on-the-spot decision-making.
> - I must let the boring things be boring and get my need for novelty, stimulation, and challenge in other areas of my life. If I don't, my brain tends to go rogue and waste time on activities that seem "productive" but aren't necessary.

Intentional Executive Functioning

Learning to live within my capacity took time and lots of trial and error. I simplified and decluttered and time blocked, but nothing helped until I got extremely intentional about my personal expectations around executive functioning.

When I gave myself permission to do *less* of the boring things of life, everything got easier. I eventually adopted a philosophy that my ADHD brain can do six or seven taxing tasks (aka the boring things I don't like) on a normal-energy day, and then I created a system where all my expectations for how I manage my home and family fit within those six or seven things.

> *Intentionally limiting my personal expectations around executive functioning is the single most effective thing that I've done to live within my capacity and to avoid burnout long term.*

I didn't start with six or seven taxing tasks and do not encourage you to start with that expectation, but if you stick with me and follow this system that I've created, you'll get there. Instead, I started with three daily tasks. As I made that my focus, I got off the chaotic roller coaster of seasons of overcommitting, followed by massive burnout. As I avoided the depletion zone and prioritized managing my ADHD, my capacity grew, and I began to have the mental and physical energy to consistently do the six or seven taxing tasks while still having margin.

This process required me to let a lot of things go that didn't really matter. Instead of wasting energy on low-priority easy tasks, I focused on getting good at the important, essential tasks of daily life that I don't enjoy but need to get done. I then gave myself permission to use the rest of my time doing stimulating, interesting, and energizing things.

I've found that through this system, though I lowered my expectations, I've increased my productivity and follow-through in every area of my life. I'm expecting myself to do fewer boring tasks but I'm able to stick to my plans and spending much less time thinking about and planning what needs to be done.

I'm also happier, calmer, more present, and much more creative. Since managing my ADHD well and making time for my interests is a central part of this strategy, every area of my life has benefited. I truly feel like I've unlocked some secret cheat code. And it's not just me. This system and strategy is literally changing the lives of so many.

You see, every time you sit down to write out a to-do list of what needs to be done in your home and life, that draws on your EF bank and burns your mental energy. Having a clear plan for your expectations means that you will spend less energy planning and have more energy to do the tasks. It's truly been life-changing for me, my family, and thousands of others using this system.

In the following chapters, I will walk you through the actionable steps to implement the Master the Mundane (MTM) system for managing your taxing tasks so that you can get out of ADHD burnout.

Taxing Tasks

The limit of six or seven taxing tasks has proved for me and thousands of others to be an incredibly helpful boundary. If my expectations for myself reside within this limit, I have enough margin to navigate the unpredictable things of life, like one of my children getting sick or a hurricane headed straight for Florida.

I think of these six or seven things as my capacity for boring or my capacity for executive functioning. It's my daily budget on high-energy days. It's important to remember that this capacity encompasses *all* of my personal life, which is why it's important to consider additional factors that might impact your own capacity.

> *By personal life, I mean all things related to taking care of myself, my kids, my home, and areas of service. I don't include my business- or work-related taxing tasks, though I'm always trying to keep that list as small as possible.*

It's important to understand what "taxing tasks" means to *you*. If you love organizing and cleaning or planning meals for your family, those may be creative outlets for you, so they wouldn't be your taxing tasks. It's essential that you get honest about what tasks you really don't enjoy. They are likely the same tasks that you consistently procrastinate about and struggle to make yourself complete.

Some seasons of life throw a lot of extra taxing tasks our way, and it's important to adjust as needed. You may have an ongoing need in your life that is very draining—such as caring for an elderly family member—that takes up one of your six or seven things. If that's the case, you may need to adjust your expectations. Similarly, you may go through a short season like a big move where you also need to pull back on your six or seven things.

The underlying assumption is that you must guard how many boring things you are expecting yourself to do daily. As new opportunities come your way, it's imperative that you consider whether it's enjoyable to you and learn to say no to any additional, unnecessary taxing tasks. Instead, invest more energy in the things you naturally enjoy and do well.

Any new circumstance that drains your executive functioning and requires planning, decision-making, organization, mental energy, and emotional energy will be extra draining to your capacity. You must adjust your expectations of yourself in those times and find ways to simplify. Expecting yourself to add more taxing tasks to your plate and stay consistent with your normal routines will leave you feeling depleted.

Circumstances That Impact Your Capacity for Taxing Tasks

- Having a baby
- Navigating illness for yourself or family member
- Selling a home or moving
- Death in the family
- Marital struggles
- Separation or divorce

When dealing with taxing circumstances, give yourself permission to adjust as needed, knowing that you have a clear plan for getting back to normal. I've found that even making this mental shift and removing the pressure makes it easier to stick to my normal six or seven tasks. Without a doubt, if you stay in your activation zone, it will be much easier to get back to normal quickly after the season ends. If you end up burned out, it will be much harder, and the taxing season will derail you.

When You Meet Friction

The fact that you are reading this book tells me that this probably isn't your first attempt to find systems and strategies to manage your home life. I've found women with ADHD to be incredibly curious people who love to learn and are constantly searching for ways to do life more effectively. I think this is extraordinarily good, but it is also one of the reasons why we often find ourselves feeling like a failure.

Yes, many of the systems that we've tried might not work for our brains, but also our curiosity is a double-edged sword. Our constant pursuit of solving problems and finding better ways of doing things often leads to wanting to recreate everything. We enjoy inventing innovative ways to solve a problem and when we meet friction or resistance, we are quick to throw our system out the window. We'd rather start over because that's more challenging and interesting.

The MTM system will help you create a strategy for managing the boring things in your life. Initially this will be fun, interesting, and energizing but ultimately, for this to stick, you must give yourself permission to let the boring things be boring and find stimulation, challenge, and fun in other ways.

But I'm going to ask you to start paying attention to that internal tendency to throw out the good and give yourself permission to go slow and focus on progress. Our goal in creating this system is to find what works for you so that you can spend less mental energy solving these problems repeatedly. If you start feeling bored and want to burn it all down and start over, that isn't a sign that this isn't working. It's most likely a sign that you are bored, possibly dysregulated, and need mental challenge or a creative outlet.

Take Your Time

I know that you will want to blow through this book and start implementing everything right away, but that isn't going to work either. I've intentionally laid this out to help you make incremental change because that has been the secret sauce to transformation for me and the thousands of women in my community. Give yourself the necessary time to implement each step and, once you've done that, move on.

There is no right pace. Once it becomes easy for *you*, it's time to add more. If life gets in the way and you get sidetracked for a few months, that's okay. Just keep going back to what you have and then add on over time. Each one of these steps will lighten your mental load and lower your daily stress.

Having a clear plan for what boring tasks are getting your time and energy will make your daily life exponentially easier. You'll be spending less energy thinking, "What do I need to?" and have less anxiety worried that you are inevitably forgetting something. Over time, as you implement the steps in this book, you will have more time and energy to do the things that help you.

This, my friend, isn't about checking off all the things on your list and doing it all perfectly, it's about learning to end the daily chaos and the stress that comes with it so that you can stop living in the depletion zone and end the ADHD burnout cycle for good.

Make This Yours

As I share each of these steps, I want to be crystal clear about one important thing. I am not advocating one right way to do life. And the goal is not for you to become me and do life just how I do it. The MTM system is a framework, but the real magic comes when you make this yours.

I can guarantee that each woman reading this book comes from a unique situation in terms of both constraints and resources. Some can afford to outsource the cleaning and others can't. Some have supportive and collaborative spouses, and others are single moms with very little support. Some have kids with very significant support needs and others don't.

It doesn't matter if you clean your own house or outsource that. It doesn't matter if your kids do travel sports and that eats up a significant amount of your time and energy. It doesn't matter if your spouse or kids help significantly with the household tasks or if they have very little capacity to do so.

> *Here's what matters:* you, *being honest about your own capacity, learning to live within your means, and learning to manage your own energy.*

Here's what matters: *you*, being honest about your own capacity, learning to live within your means, and learning to manage your own energy. Your taxing tasks will be different from others. How this all works in your life will be different. The goal is to give you a framework to identify your core needs so you can then live those out.

This work is about *you*. Whatever doesn't fit in your life and can't be outsourced or delegated, you need to let go of for right now. Instead of trying to make the puzzle pieces fit, this work is about actively simplifying and clarifying your expectations of yourself for this current season of life.

Moving Out of Chaos

As you follow the steps, you will be led away from a chaotic pace of daily life to calmer days, calmer weeks, calmer months, and then calmer seasons.

What do I mean by chaos? I'd describe chaos as living in burnout and/or consistently trying to function in the depletion zone. It's where you are consistently living outside of your executive functioning capacity, and you don't have the mental energy to address the small tasks of life.

Small decisions and tasks—like what's for dinner, where are the clean socks, or who is picking up the kids—feel overwhelming and cause unnecessary stress on you, your spouse, and the rest of your family. It's incredibly stressful if you've been living this way for a long time, and creating these systems will be life changing.

Getting out of chaos requires slowly creating margin so that when life happens, we have the capacity to deal with it. We can stay regulated and have the mental clarity to navigate the daily challenges of life and parenthood.

MOVING OUT OF CHAOS

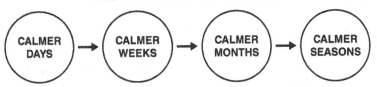

An essential part of this requires that you give yourself permission to start small and build from there. There is a major ADHD tendency to want to overcomplicate things and create a system that addresses every possible problem in our lives at once but is then impossible to implement. We aren't going to do that.

Instead, we are going to focus on moving away from chaos by first focusing on our days, then our weeks, then our months, and then eventually our seasons. As you create structure and routines through each step of this process, your daily stress and your mental load will decrease and you will create more margin.

Lasting Change Takes Intentionality

If you're following these steps and thinking, "This seems like a lot of work" and hoping for an easier way to figure this all out, I feel you.

I'd love nothing more than to sell you an easy-to-duplicate tool that would alleviate all your ADHD struggles. But I'm guessing that you've already bought everything on the market and after a few days realized that it wasn't going to help you.

I myself have many half-completed planners, and every time I open them up and see that I gave up on the habit after a few days, I feel so discouraged and frustrated. You see, any tool that requires you to fill it out each day and create a to-do list or a clean plan of action

(continued)

(continued)

for your time and energy is draining your mental energy before you even get started. And since our mental energy is inconsistent, it's unwise for us to plan for this energy to show up every day. We need to do everything in our power to plan around our struggles and accommodate them by creating tools and systems that don't require executive functioning each day.

Though this work will require mental energy and intentionality, it will make your days, weeks and months so much smoother. And, as I've found time and time again, my brain does so much better with bulk planning than it does with planning for small periods of time. Though to some it may seem harder, it's much easier for my brain because my ADHD brain loves challenge.

These systems are designed to serve you on a long-term basis and will help you create more capacity so that your daily life will be less stressful and less chaotic. It will take work, but this work is incredibly rewarding. It will mean less stress, less anxiety, and a less shame.

I make small tweaks to my system with each new season, but those are very minimal. The idea is that as you do this work, you are creating a system that you can use forever so that you can stop wasting energy coming up with an entirely new system for how you manage your life every six months. The time you put into this will come back to you tenfold, I promise!

As you start this process, I encourage you to reflect on *why* you want to have less stress and chaos when it comes to your daily life and your family. Take some time to get a clear picture of what it will look and feel like when you aren't living in burnout. How will your family life be impacted? How will your personal goals be impacted? How will your marriage be impacted? How will your mental health be impacted? How will your children be impacted?

Hold on to that image and come back to it if you get discouraged in this process.

Step 1: Identify Your Daily Three

Trust me that I know that you have more than three things that you want to accomplish on any given day. But identifying your three daily tasks is imperative for three reasons:

1. ADHD brains tend to forget what we do accomplish, which often leaves us feeling defeated and unproductive. Having a clear daily three will help you get better at celebrating what you *do* accomplish. And ADHD brains thrive on positive reinforcement.
2. Having a clear daily three is incredibly helpful on low-energy days when your brain is struggling with executive function. Pausing to think, "What do I need to do?" burns mental energy, and on low-energy days we need to hold our EFs in reserve. Having a clear plan means less planning and decision-making and less executive functioning.
3. Finally, having a clear daily three that is easy enough for you to maintain and addresses your most essential daily struggles will prevent your home from getting completely overwhelming. Attending to your daily three won't mean that your home is perfectly clean, but you will avoid that tipping point where your home feels out of control and you feel paralyzed to take action.

For me, this tipping point looks like two to three days' worth of dirty dishes in the sink and clutter throughout the home on the floors. Dirty laundry and dirty towels have piled up, and there is likely trash and dirty cups scattered throughout. When my home is in this state of disrepair, it's stressful for me and I get very dysregulated. When I'm dysregulated, it's then hard to take action to get my home back together. And when my home is like this, it requires a lot of effort to get it back in order.

Your daily three is the three clear actions that you can take consistently that are realistic and attainable and keep you from reaching your tipping point. If you

Your daily three is the three clear actions that you can take each day that are realistic and attainable and keep you from reaching your tipping point.

do these things daily, your home will feel manageable, and your days will feel less stressful. These three tasks should be easy enough that they can be done in less than one hour.

I will share my daily three, but I think it's important for you to decide what is most helpful to you and your family. Your spouse or child may unload the dishwasher, for example, so that may not be relevant for you. It's important that your daily three be personalized to your family's most basic needs. Your daily three should be just tasks that you expect yourself to do.

It is helpful to address your daily three at the time of day where your energy is the highest. For me, that's the morning so I do my daily three tasks in the morning. I usually sprinkle them throughout my morning with the aim of having them done before I leave the house to take the kids to school. I don't stress about them happening at the same time or in the same order.

My Daily Three

One Load of Laundry
I start a load of laundry while my tea brews and move it to the dryer while the kids eat breakfast. I move the dry clothes to our large laundry hamper at some point during the day or the following morning. I don't try to fold them or put them away.

Clean Dishes and Tidy the Kitchen
I unload the dishwasher, load the dirty dishes into the dishwasher, and get to an empty sink. I then declutter the kitchen counters and wipe them all down. It doesn't stay this way long but if I can do this once a day, it remains manageable.

Plan for Meals for that Day
I make breakfast, decide what I will eat for lunch, and decide on what we will have dinner. This usually looks like grabbing something out of the freezer to defrost and pulling out what I need from the pantry. I make sure that we have everything needed on hand for dinner ready to go. I can't commit to a week's worth of meals but deciding the day of works for me. In seasons past, I've also made my kids lunch at this time, but they have since taken that over themselves.

If you aren't sure what to pick, I encourage you to try my daily three and then tweak them as needed. You might edit your daily three a few times at first until you determine what three tasks are most helpful to you. This is what you think of as the bare minimum and is very likely things you are already doing but not currently giving yourself credit for.

As you shift your focus to your daily three tasks, practice being proud of yourself for completing these three tasks. As someone with a brain that hates doing boring monotonous tasks, you must celebrate and reward yourself for doing these tasks. The sooner you learn to be your own cheerleader for completing your daily three, the easier it will be to add more.

I also highly encourage you to print a physical checklist because that will give you an extra dopamine boost. Take a selfie with your checklist and tag me on social media so that I can celebrate your progress.

> *"The daily three allowed me to trust myself again. I knew I had a base system I could fall back on if something derailed me, like an emergency happened or a big project took over. I didn't have to worry about being overwhelmed on where to start because I already had made that decision and had a plan. I had already proven its worth by doing it every day in the calm moments and having it be my foundation piece."*
>
> *MTM Community Member*

Step 1 Application: Determine your daily three.

Tip: Create a physical checklist to mark off these three tasks each day. Go to the book resource page found at https://www.amymariehann.com/mtmbook to download, edit and print a free template.

My Daily Three

4

Master the Fundamentals

The fact that you are reading this book tells me this isn't your first rodeo in terms of trying to create routine and structure for you and your family. I'm just going to assume that you know that you need routine and structure and you know what habits you "should" be doing to take better care of yourself. Friend, I know that you don't need any more guilt piled on top of your already overloaded shoulders.

As I began to see that so many of my daily motherhood struggles were really ADHD struggles, it was clear that I had to prioritize my brain health and the needs of my ADHD brain to overcome them. If I wanted to be on top of the boring things of daily life and manage my emotions and be a present mom to my kids, I had to make time for the big needs of my ADHD brain. How could I expect my brain to behave differently if I wasn't giving it what it needed to function?

And yet this revelation was also incredibly annoying. Managing my own mental health kind of felt like a full-time job. And I really wanted an easier, quicker strategy that I could implement right away.

Despite my annoyance, I was so desperate that eventually I went all in on this theory, and it has paid off immensely. Learning to manage my ADHD well

> "I sure notice when I am neglecting my self-care. I am less productive, miss taking my medication, eat poorly, and struggle with the smallest of tasks. When I sleep, eat, and take my meds correctly, I am usually more productive and feel like I can manage my day more efficiently and easily. I find more joy in my day and in others."
>
> MTM Community Member

and to design a life that takes my needs and my kids needs into consideration is truly the only thing that has worked for me and has proven to help so many others.

I get that you might want to jump right to the practical strategies for managing your home and family. But friend, if you don't first learn to manage your ADHD, you'll be stuck in the cycle of shame and overwhelm chasing the dopamine from random projects and distractions. You'll stay on the burnout roller coaster and won't get to the root of your struggles or find long-term change.

For years I thought that my ADHD was fully managed by taking medicine. I thought that if I took my medicine, I'd be able to keep up with my peers in every area of life. And though I still do take ADHD medication and believe that is life-changing for many, it is just one piece of the puzzle of what it looks like to manage my ADHD well.

Medication alone was not enough for me, and I had so many ADHD struggles that were holding me back in significant ways. Real change happened for me when I learned to live within my capacity *and* learned to proactively manage my ADHD.

I don't just mean that my house got cleaner or that I yelled at the kids less (though that did happen). I mean I launched the business that I'd dreamed about and increased my income by 10-fold even though I'm working less. I mean I finally conquered habits like overdrinking and overeating that plagued me for years. I mean that my home became calm and peaceful on a (mostly) daily basis and I'm able to spend much less time on the boring things. I mean that my marriage is stronger than it has ever been. I mean I am healthier and happier and more confident in every area of my life than I can ever remember being.

> *I've learned that when I'm living within my capacity and intentionally managing my ADHD, everything in life gets easier.*

Going all in on my hunch has paid off big time. Even though it's a scary shift if you are used to living from a place of perfectionism and overcompensation, I'm going to ask you to trust me on this one.

All-or-Nothing Thinking

For years I made an enormous mistake every time I'd try to get my life together, which in fact kept me stuck. Like so many with ADHD, I was trapped in all-or-nothing thinking and would create these elaborate systems that addressed every area of my life at once in one fell swoop.

It sounded something like this:

- I'm going to start waking up at 5 every morning to go to the gym for 45 minutes of weights, 30 minutes of cardio, and then sit in the sauna for 20 minutes.
- I'm then going to come home and make myself a green smoothie because I'm going to cut out caffeine for good.
- I'm going to finally ditch gluten and sugar and get the kids off their macaroni and cheese addiction.
- We are going to stop using any screens during the week because I'm sick and tired of their cranky attitudes.

These elaborate plans would rarely stick for even 24 hours because, despite my own desires, I am not in fact a robot. I can't reprogram every one of my settings on a random Tuesday evening. Real, lasting change, especially for someone with ADHD, takes time and intentionality.

And here's the thing. None of these changes in themselves are bad, but no one can change all these things at once, and trying to do so will leave you feeling like a failure.

I've made incredible strides in my health, my parenting, and my business, but I haven't yet fully figured out any of those changes I just mentioned. Yes, they sound great, but you'll never find me telling you to do anything that I haven't personally implemented consistently in to my own life.

Slow and Steady

Though it's incredibly important for you to learn to prioritize the needs of your brain, the pace at which you expect yourself to change is also incredibly important. ADHD brains function so much better when we have routine, structure, systems, and predictability. And yet we also have this unrealistic expectation that we can transform our lives at the drop of a hat, which is what keeps us stuck.

Instead, we are going to take the slow and steady approach, focusing on small tweaks to the areas of your life that will help you the most so that you can stop feeling like a failure and start seeing progress. Small progress over time leads to massive change when you learn to implement and integrate these changes into your everyday life.

As we continue to take the slow and steady approach to create sustainable structure for our days, the next step is to get a clear plan for what it looks like to manage the fundamentals. In future steps, we'll add more structure to this plan that will feel more like a daily routine, but taking each step at a time is what will make this doable for you.

The Fundamentals

Every time I open Instagram, I'm bombarded with new "self-care strategies" from red light masks to weighted vests to cold plunges. The list goes on and on. And though I love a new gadget or health hack as much as the next gal, I'm a busy mom and my time and energy are limited. I didn't need a longer list of things to do to improve my ADHD struggles; I needed clarity on what mattered most and permission to focus on fewer things.

I needed to narrow it down to the fundamentals that I could incorporate them into my daily life. So I focused on what made the biggest difference to my energy level, brain function, and family. This came down to the three basics: self-care, stimulation, and parenting.

THE FUNDAMENTALS

Self-Care
- Sleep
- Nutrition
- Exercise
- Emotional Regulation

Stimulation
- Mental Challenge
- Novelty/Fun
- Creative Outlets

Parenting
- Connection
- Nutrition
- Exercise
- Special Interests

Embracing each of these three categories as equally important in managing ADHD for me and my family has meant needing to get strategic around my expectations of myself in each of these categories.

The self-care habits that help those with ADHD are helpful for all people. Are there additional things that you can do to help improve your mental health? Yes, but the intention of this book isn't to impress you with all of my ADHD knowledge. It's to give you real, practical advice to help you as a busy mom. And I believe the self-care basics of sleep, nutrition, exercise, and emotional regulation are the most important needs to address.

In addition, ADHD brains need stimulation on a regular basis to function. We need challenge but we also need novelty, connection, and creative outlets. Stimulation isn't a fun bonus; it's an essential need that must be met for us to stay on top of the taxing tasks of daily life. Without stimulation, your brain will continue to go rogue, seeking dopamine in nonurgent projects, and you'll stay stuck on the burnout roller coaster.

> *Stimulation isn't a fun bonus; it's an essential need that must be met for us to stay on top of the taxing tasks of daily life.*

In addition, as moms raising kids with ADHD, we must also prioritize helping our kids proactively meet these same needs. If managing *our* ADHD is essential to us being able to do the boring things in life, then helping our kids manage *their* ADHD is essential to them being able to do their boring things in life. If we aren't also keeping their needs top of mind, their struggles will make our daily lives significantly harder. There will be more discipline and behavior issues, sibling fighting, and chaos in our homes.

> *Learning to thrive with ADHD for me has meant treating these three core needs as fundamental and necessary parts of my life and designing a life that prioritizes them.*

Habit Focus

For step 2, I'm going to ask you to identify three core daily habits for each of the fundamental areas. The goal here is that you let go of the ideal "all-or-nothing" plan where you perfectly master each of these areas. Instead, I want you to think about where you are and determine what progress looks like in these areas.

You may already exercise consistently or sleep like a rock star or be a meal prep machine. We all come from different places in our journeys and have different areas that need our focused attention. As you read the next bit, think about what progress in these areas looks like for you as I ask you to clarify one habit goal for each area.

Sleep

Sleep is essential to everyone but imperative to those of us with ADHD brains. Unfortunately, it can also be incredibly challenging for many of us to both go to bed and to sleep deeply.

I've always loved sleep and needed a lot of it. I'm naturally an early bird and my brain works best in the morning. I can remember in high school and college regularly going to bed before 10 p.m. and getting up early. I think my personal ideal sleep hours would be 10 p.m.–7 a.m. every night if I didn't have to worry about anyone else.

Many ADHDers are wired differently and prefer to stay up late and struggle to get up early in the morning. I'm a big believer that fighting against your natural tendencies is a huge waste of energy. It's much more productive to be honest about your natural tendencies and lean in to find ways to support your natural rhythms than to expect yourself to change completely.

I don't care what time you go to bed and what time you get up. This isn't a productivity book where I'm going to tell you that you need to wake up at 5 a.m. to be a productive and successful adult and shame you if that is not how you are wired. If you consistently struggle getting enough sleep, I encourage you to focus first on this one essential thing.

To improve your sleep, you need to first get clear on your personal sleep fundamentals.

Sleep Fundamentals

- How many hours of sleep does your brain need to function at its best?
- How much time do you need to wind down at night to fall asleep?
- What is your ideal time to fall asleep?

- What time do you need to start winding down so that you can fall asleep at your ideal time?
- What is your ideal time to wake up so that you can get enough sleep?

Once you are clear on those, you can learn ways to get better at winding down, going to sleep at your ideal time, and then waking up at your ideal time.

My Sleep Fundamentals

- I need eight to nine hours of sleep.
- I need two hours to wind down from the day to fall asleep.
- I want to fall asleep by 10 p.m. and get up by 6 a.m. so that I can have one hour to myself before my kids need me in the morning.
- I need to start winding down for bedtime at 8 p.m. to fall asleep by 10 p.m.

Your Turn:

- *I need _____ hours of sleep.*
- *I need _____ hours to wind down from the day to fall asleep.*
- *I want to fall asleep by _____ and get up at _____ on a consistent basis.*
- *I need to start winding down for bed at _____ in order to fall asleep by _____.*

Now that you have a clear idea of your sleep *goal,* you can work on making tweaks to your life to help you live this out. I wish I could tell you that you are a robot and that your settings are easily reprogrammed to start implementing this new protocol, but it's much more complicated than that.

Once I turned 40, getting good sleep became a lot more complicated, and getting consistent sleep now requires a lot of intentionality. I also still have young kids who often crawl in my bed in the middle of the night. There are many things outside of my control, but I've realized that to get good sleep, I must be intentional about those things that I can control.

Many moms I talk with stay up much later than they want to because it's the first time that they have allowed themselves to do anything fun or stimulating. Basically, they can't fall asleep because their brains are bored after a day spent doing boring things. Learning to make room for mental stimulation and interest throughout your day is essential in breaking this cycle.

Exercise

Exercise has transformative effects on our brains' ability to perform executive functioning. If your daily struggles in life are rooted in your executive functioning ability, exercise is proven to improve these struggles by increasing dopamine and norepinephrine. It is by far one of the most therapeutic things we can do to manage our ADHD.

I'm going to go out on a limb and suggest that this isn't new information. I'm going to assume that if you aren't currently exercising regularly, you already know the benefits of exercise but your challenges with exercise are in lacking the time or the motivation to exercise consistently. So let's focus on helping in those two areas.

I'll admit that I really enjoy exercise. I am not especially coordinated and don't enjoy group or team sports, but I've always liked going to the gym and trying new things. For me, exercise is fun, but I get that it's a lot more complicated if you fundamentally don't enjoy exercise.

Exercise has looked so many ways for me as a mom. There were many years where we couldn't afford a gym membership and many years where I could barely get 15 minutes by myself. But as I look back over the years, there are a few major mindset shifts that have helped me to make exercise a consistent part of my life.

Shift One: Accepting That Exercise Is a Nonnegotiable

Exercise is my main emotional release and is essential for my mental health. I struggle falling asleep if I haven't been moving my body. My executive functioning struggles are much worse if I'm not exercising regularly. Even if I don't have the energy for a long walk, I've tried to embrace that something is better than nothing. A 10-minute jump on the trampoline or splashing around in the pool with the kids is better than not moving at all and will still improve my mood and sleep.

Shift Two: Focusing on How I Feel Versus How I Look

Exercising consistently became so much easier when I took weight loss off the table and let my focus for getting exercise be for my mental health and how it makes me feel. I spent many years obsessing about calories and weight, but when I let the goal of my workouts be to feel my best and not for scale-based victories, they became so much more enjoyable.

Instead of using the scale to measure my progress or success, I focus on how my exercise habits are impacting my sleep, my mood, and my creativity. I've identified that I fall asleep the easiest when I am getting around 10,000 steps a day and I'm calmer and more focused when I'm lifting heavy weights three or four times a week.

For me, this mindset shift really helped break down the motivation barrier. If my goal for working out is just to lose weight, that doesn't keep me motivated to keep at it when I'm not seeing results. But if my goal is to be calmer and to have more mental and physical energy *today*, it's much more motivating to exercise *today*.

Shift Three: Stopped Masking My Need for Movement

As I began to really understand my ADHD struggles, it became clear that my overeating and overdrinking struggles were coping strategies that I used for years to mask my internal hyperactivity. It felt more socially acceptable to refill my cup or to grab another cookie than to admit that I was antsy and needed to go for a walk or stretch my legs.

Breaking those habits required me to get honest with my body's need for movement and stimulation and to find healthy, productive ways to meet those needs. My body struggles to sit still and if I'm going to sit at a desk for more than three hours or watch a long movie or sit through my son's soccer game or attend a boring PTA meeting without self-medicating, then I'm going to need to have gotten hard exercise.

Shift Four: Gave Myself Permission to Let Each Day Look Different

I've had many different exercise routines over the years, but I can tell you with absolute certainty that having a week where every day looks the same is very rare. I'd love to tell you that I wake up every day at 5 a.m. to go to the gym but that has happened maybe two weeks in my whole life. *Every* day of anything is an unrealistic goal for me because my energy fluctuates.

If early mornings are the best time for you to exercise, try setting your alarm every morning but make your goal to go to the gym two mornings a week. If you get to the gym and work out two mornings out of the five days in the week, count that as a success. Start small and then as your body adjusts and if you get better at getting out of bed, than maybe shift your expectation to three mornings and then maybe even four mornings.

I'm currently going to the gym three or four days a week, with my preference being for going from 6 to 7 a.m. If I don't make it out of the house for that, I go after I take my oldest to school or even in the late afternoon before I pick him up. If I don't get to the gym enough times during the week, then I go to the gym on Saturday or Sunday, which I've found that I really enjoy because I get a little break from the kids and the gym is quieter on those days. Basically, I get to the gym consistently, but *when* I get there is a little all over the place.

Sticking to the exact same daily schedule isn't my goal. Getting enough exercise is my goal and if I'm doing that, I consider it a win. I've learned that expecting myself to do anything the same way *every* day is unrealistic and unsustainable for me.

Shift Five: Embracing What I Actually Enjoy

Exercise can look so many ways, and I've learned to embrace what I really enjoy and to ignore what doesn't work for me.

Your exercise likes and preferences may be completely different from mine and that's okay. I encourage you to be honest about what *you* enjoy, what helps you the most, and what goals are realistic for you in this current season of life. Whatever exercise goals you set for yourself, make sure that they are based on *your* actual preferences.

Lack of time may still be a struggle but creating a vision of exercise that you *enjoy* and *want* to do removes a huge barrier.

This might look like:

- Is tracking steps a helpful metric to you? If so, how many steps would you like to get in a day?
- Do you prefer to exercise alone or with others?

- Do you prefer to exercise in nature, at home, or in a gym?
- Do you prefer to listen to music or to have a guided workout?
- Do you like to have flexibility about when you work out or do you need a set class time for accountability?
- Do you like to have a schedule or routine to follow or to do your own thing?
- Realistically, how many times a week would you ideally like to exercise to feel your best?

When you have a clear sense of what form of exercise is the most realistic, accessible, and enjoyable for you, identify one specific daily habit you'd like to pursue around exercise.

This might look like:

- I will incorporate movement into my normal life by tracking my steps. My goal is to increase my daily step count to 7,000 steps/day. I'm going to buy a walking pad to walk while I work.
- I will walk my dogs one mile a day.
- I will go to the gym for 45 minutes or go for a walk in my neighborhood for 45 minutes.
- I will do a yoga video or go on a walk every day for 20–30 minutes.

Your Turn:

My Exercise-Related Daily Habit:

Nutrition

Food can feel so complicated, and the reality is that it requires a lot of executive functioning and planning to feed yourself and your kids. What has helped me and my family the most is to focus on the basics and pursue change slowly.

For years I would try and go gung-ho for changing our diets. I would try and go cold turkey with some paleo diet plan and try and change everything at once and that would become completely overwhelming for me. I'd try and make all these healthy meals my family wouldn't eat and end up feeling like a failure.

But as I focused on stopping the compulsive overeating, I realized that many of my struggles were based on not eating enough. I started tracking my calories a few years ago, not with the intent of losing weight but to get a feel for how much I was eating.

I'd consistently be starving in the evening and binge on sugar or alcohol because I hadn't eaten enough during the day. When I started getting better at eating a good breakfast and a good lunch, my cravings and compulsive overeating subsided. I also had more energy and was in a better mood during the day.

Eating consistently is an important first step in learning to manage your ADHD. Give yourself permission to make small changes over time instead of trying to change everything at once. As you look at where you are today with your habits around nutrition, identify one specific habit that would help you make progress in this area of managing your ADHD.

This might look like:

- Start eating breakfast before work or taking the kids to school.
- Start packing breakfast and lunch to take to work.
- Make a filling, protein-filled lunch.
- Eat a hearty snack or make a smoothie in the late afternoon.

Your Turn:

My Nutrition-Related Daily Habit:

Emotional Regulation

Learning to regulate your emotions as an adult with ADHD is an ongoing effort and may require working with a counselor or therapist. I'll talk about this in more detail in Chapter 9, but as you move out of burnout, I encourage you to find a healthy outlet for emotional release. It is a very normal part of ADHD to have big feelings and big reactions. What are you actively doing to process and release those big emotions so that they don't become rage or lead to self-sabotage?

Intense exercise, verbally processing with a friend or therapist, journaling, a creative hobby, and dancing to music are all healthy emotional outlets to help you release your pent-up emotional energy. These outlets also provide space for you to process your actions and behaviors and to reflect on why a certain situation may have triggered you.

As you begin to structure your life around managing your ADHD, what daily habit might you intentionally pursue to serve as an emotional check-in and release?

This might look like:

- I will spend five minutes journaling while drinking my coffee.
- I will listen to a meditation or reflection every morning before looking at social media.
- I will talk about my day for 10 minutes every day with my spouse after the kids go to bed.
- I will call my mom and process my day every morning on the way to work.
- I will have a daily dance party or go on a run to release emotions from the day.

Your Turn:

My Daily Habit for Emotional Release:

Challenge

If you are in the boredom zone, it may very well be because you are understimulated and deeply needing challenge. And yet it can be so perplexing to know how to pursue challenge when you have very little time and energy to give.

I'm guessing that, like me, you have many small challenges that you'd love to tackle. You know, things like learning to master making sourdough bread on a weekly basis or learning to play pickleball. For years I spread myself thin over lots of small challenges and never felt like I was making much progress.

I have learned that it's far more productive and energizing in the long run to focus my mental energy on pursuing one big challenge at a time. I still have small hobbies and creative outlets, but I think of those more as the novelty/fun aspect of my life.

Currently, my big challenge is writing this book. There are many other big challenges on my radar, like launching a podcast, writing a cookbook, and creating a second course, but this endeavor is filling my need for challenge and taking all my extra capacity right now. The list of future projects is continuously growing and when this challenge is over, I will pick one from that list for my next big challenge.

It's imperative that your outlet for mental challenge be something that you deeply enjoy and find fulfilling. There are "challenges" that are boring and draining and leave you absolutely depleted. That's not the good kind of challenge your brain needs.

You are looking for the kind of challenge that you will think about in the small mundane moments of your day until you crack it. If you were locked in a room with this challenge and your laptop, you'd be absolutely delighted to hyperfocus on this challenge for 48 hours straight. This should be a challenge that you don't just feel like you "should" figure out but that you desperately want to pursue out of your own curiosity.

If you work full-time, I encourage you to think about this challenge as the piece of your job that you most enjoy. Even in professions we love, it's easy to get caught up in meetings and emails, but we need to block off time for the projects that we find the most challenging and fulfilling even if it's only one hour a day. It might also look like pursuing additional education or training or taking on a new research project.

As you identify your area of challenge, consider how you might break up your progress over the course of a week. For example, if you're using naptime every day to pursue your area of challenge, it would help to have a clear goal for each week that you could break into four or five weekly tasks that you can complete throughout the week. It's important to be realistic about your actual capacity and to feel like you are making progress.

Challenge

Launch a Blog

WEEKLY SUBTASKS:

Write New Blog Post	Edit Post + Add Photos	Post to Pinterest + SEO	Create Social Media Posts	Weekly Newsletter

This might look like:

- Taking a class or course to learn a specific skill
- Launching some kind of business endeavor
- Planning a project or event
- Starting or joining a social club or team
- Pursuing a research project or idea
- A specific project around your house

Identify your one area of challenge for this current season of life. If you aren't clear on what challenge you want to pursue, lean heavily into novelty/fun as your outlet for stimulation for the time being. You will get greater clarity on your areas of challenge over time.

Your Turn:

My Current Area of Challenge:

Novelty and Fun

ADHD brains are interest driven. We get energized by the things *we* like and enjoy, not by the things that we think we are *supposed* to like and enjoy.

Learning to be honest about what I like, enjoy, and think is fun and then making time for those things has been truly life changing. Not only did it get so much easier to do the boring things of daily life, but I stopped wasting time and energy on random nonurgent projects because my need for novelty was already met. It got so much easier to ignore my random ideas, which meant that I wasn't getting sidetracked all the time.

> *We get energized by the things* we *like and enjoy, not by the things that we think we are* supposed *to like and enjoy.*

I also gave myself permission to sprinkle in fun to my daily life as much as possible.

> *If I'm doing the dishes, I'm probably watching* Gilmore Girls *on my phone.*
>
> *If I'm watching a movie with my kids, I'm probably painting a picture or doing a puzzle at the same time.*
>
> *If I'm doing yard work, I'm probably listening to '90s hip-hop and slightly gyrating as I go.*
>
> *If I'm on a walk, I'm probably listening to a podcast that makes me laugh.*

If you're thinking, "I have no idea what I think is fun!" you aren't alone. It's a common sentiment from every mom I work with in my coaching program.

Learning what you find fun and enjoy in your current season of your life is a big part of the self-discovery journey. There are things you might have pursued in earlier seasons of your life that are much harder to pursue in your current constraints, so we must find new things that we can incorporate in our lives in a way that works.

> *"Across the two years I've been in MTM, I have set up my week to have daily time for what I love—writing—six days a week. This has been amazing and is like an ongoing fruit of the program."*
> — MTM Community Member

For example, before I had kids, my favorite hobby was spending an entire Saturday driving out to a flea market in the country with my girlfriends. I love being able to unplug from everything, see all the things, be in the sunshine, and have long meandering conversations. I still very much love doing all these things, but this is incredibly hard for me to pull off in this current season of life. And if I could pull it off, my girlfriends are just as busy as I am and can't drop everything to go with me like we could in our 20s.

Instead, I've found that mini-hobbies are a much better fit for me in this season of life. Focus on mini-hobbies and give yourself permission to have a lot of them. Resist the temptation to find the "one thing" that will be "your thing" because that will make you feel like a failure. You will be more satisfied if you have one big stimulating challenge and a lot of small mini-hobbies.

A mini-hobby shouldn't be a huge financial investment. Don't go buy every supply that has ever existed for this new hobby. That will make it more stressful because you will feel like you must stick to it for a certain amount of time. The whole point of the mini-hobby is novelty and fun and not for it to be one more thing for you to feel bad about. If your fascination with the mini-hobby only lasts for a week or two, that is totally okay.

The possibilities are endless for finding mini-hobbies but I do encourage you to look for things that are away from screens, especially if you are frequently overstimulated. If your go-to activity when you have a few minutes to yourself is to scroll on your phone, you need a mini-hobby to replace it. Think about mini-hobbies as something that you can you fit into pockets of time lasting 5 to 20 minutes.

Examples of Mini-Hobbies

Paint-by-number kit
Listening to a podcast series
Reading a fun book series
Bingeing a fun show
Doing a new puzzle
Reading books from the library
Styling an outfit from your closet with things you already have

Organizing an area of your home
Making a new recipe
Making or editing a video of a family outing
Needlepoint or cross-stitch
Trying a new kind of exercise
Learning a new card game
Painting a piece of furniture
Planning a playdate or social outing
Taking a craft or artistic class

When to Fit Mini-Hobbies into Your Day

During naptime
While doing boring daily tasks
During kid activities
Waiting in the car line
During your lunch break
While commuting on public transportation
While waiting for appointments
Between clients
After your kids go to sleep
Date night with your spouse
Moms' night out with a friend

I promise you that your brain will be more energized to do the boring things of life when you are intentionally making time for the things you enjoy.

If you've been programmed to think that you need to be super productive every hour of your day, this suggestion may sound totally silly and indulgent. I promise you that your brain will be more energized to do the boring things of life when you are intentionally making time for the things you enjoy. Incorporating mini-hobbies into your daily life will make it exponentially easier to do your taxing tasks.

Since I know that your mom guilt might get in the way of making this a reality, I want you to get strategic and intentional about how you plan to make time for novelty and fun. As you move to the next step, I want you to identify one or two specific ways that you will incorporate novelty and fun into your daily life.

This might look like:

- Make time daily for reading for pleasure during your lunch break, during your kid's activities, and after they go to bed.
- Listen to a fun podcast or book on the way to work or while waiting in the car line.
- Watch a fun show while eating lunch.
- Make time for your current craft project during naptime or while watching a show with your spouse after the kids are in bed.

Your Turn:

My Daily Habits for Novelty + Fun:

Parenting

As the mom of three kids with ADHD, it often feels like a never-ending game of whack-a-mole. As soon as one area of concern with one child gets addressed, something else pops up that needs my attention. And round and round it goes.

I'm a huge believer that we need to parent our kids differently and that the big needs of our kids matter. But also, friend, I get that it's a lot.

And if you are coming out of a season of significant ADHD burnout and trying to create structure and routine for your family after years of trying and failing, I'm going to encourage you to let that be the focus. I'm a firm believer that learning to manage your own ADHD is one of the best things that you can do to serve and support your neurodivergent kids. Choosing to let that be your focus isn't the same thing as neglecting your kids' needs, and this work will improve your ability to support your kids in a big way.

That also doesn't mean that you can just completely write off supporting your kids with ADHD. Instead, I encourage you to major in the majors when it comes to parenting your kids.

ADHD Parenting Majors

- Are they getting enough to eat to avoid hangry energy crashes?
- Are they getting enough exercise?
- Are they getting enough sleep?
- Are you intentionally connecting with them one-on-one each day?

And the reality is that though this list is super simplified, I fully understand that navigating these four basics might feel daunting. So give yourself permission to focus initially on developing daily habits that support these major needs. Let go of perfection and focus on progress. And if you can only pick one, let it be connection.

The Basics

There are so many great books about parenting kids with ADHD and I've gleaned so much over the years, but when it comes to how I live life day in and day out, prioritizing the basics has been the most helpful.

Keeping these needs top of mind daily is the only way that I have found to support my kids well consistently. Because for me, the problem isn't in the knowing what to do; it's in the doing.

For example, after school has always been hard for my kids. They struggle to eat lunch, so they come home hangry, cranky, and dysregulated. They need a snack right away and then a window of time to relax before we do anything.

Often when they are dysregulated after school, they will forget to eat a snack. I must remind them right away to eat something or their bad mood persists, and our afternoon and evening can easily go off the rails. And yet I struggled with having a snack ready for them and then also reminding them for years.

As I have adopted small daily habits to support them around their basic needs for exercise, nutrition, and sleep, our days have become much more peaceful. I've personally found that if my kids have eaten enough and gotten enough exercise, sleep is a natural byproduct.

Prioritizing these habits as essential to the well-being of our family also helped me block out the appropriate amount of time for these needs. I now know that my kids don't do well with activities right after school. I also know that bedtime goes best when we are all home by 8 p.m. This information has impacted the activities and commitments we make on an ongoing basis.

What daily habits might help you make progress in addressing these three basic needs of your children?

This might look like:

- Have a hearty afternoon snack ready after school.
- On days with no after school activities, stop at the playground for 45 minutes after school pick up.
- Start the bedtime routine by 7:30 p.m. so everyone is asleep by 9:00 p.m.

Your Turn:

One Daily Habit to Support Your Children's Nutrition Needs:

One Daily Habit to Support Your Children's Exercise Needs:

One Daily Habit to Support Your Children's Sleep Needs:

These habits should be specific and focused on progress. Start small. It will likely take you time to fully adopt these habits so I'm not suggesting you will be able to implement them all perfectly right away but, they should be realistic and measurable.

Connection

I'm going to define connection as giving our children our undivided attention for 10–20 minutes. During this time, we aren't trying to correct or discipline them. We aren't multitasking. We aren't on our phones and, ideally, our phones are in a different room. We are fully present and giving our children control of the situation. Our children get to choose what we do and how we play.

Connection is important for all children, but it's especially effective for kids with ADHD who receive massive amounts of correction throughout the day. I believe that this intentional focused time is the single most effective habit we can nurture in ourselves as parents. I'm not alone in this and didn't make it up.

> Dr. Russell Barkley encourages parents in *12 Principles for Raising a Child with ADHD* to "set aside 15–20 minutes each day as a special time to play with, attend to, approve of, acknowledge, appreciate and otherwise be mindful of your child as she is at that moment."
>
> Dr. Becky Kennedy advises parents in *Good Inside* that "Play No Phone Time [her name for this type of connection] is the parenting strategy that I recommend most often. When it comes to bang for your buck, nothing else even comes close."
>
> Dr. Mark Bertin encourages parents in *Mindful Parenting for ADHD*, "Commit to giving each of your children your full attention once a day. Schedule at least 15 minutes of together time. During this time, focus fully on your child as best as you can."

I find that right before bed is the easiest time for me and for my children to make time for this type of connection. If I'm mentally and physically tired, it's easier for me to sit still and to give them my full attention in their activity of choice. It's also a helpful reward to them for getting ready for bed and has a clear ending time, which makes it easier for me.

For example, if my daughter takes her bath and gets ready for bed by 7:45 p.m., we can play Barbies together for 15 minutes before we start reading. I set a reoccurring alarm on my phone so that she knows if she is ready for bed when that goes off, she gets this time with Mommy. I'm not bringing up a situation from earlier in the day in attempt to address some parenting concern. I'm present to play, encourage, and offer approval wherever possible.

Side note: If you aren't making time for stimulation and rest during the day, this likely won't work. You're going to be anxious to get the children to bed so that you can finally do something fun and won't be able to give them your presence. Making time for my interests during the day was a key part of being able to engage in play before bed.

If connection doesn't come easily to you, you aren't alone and you don't need to be ashamed. Be honest about where you are and find ways to make progress in finding meaningful ways to give your children your undivided attention. You are allowed to be a work in progress and just because it feels awkward or hard today doesn't mean that it always will.

If I'm not thinking about connection as an intentional habit that I need to plan for, it won't happen. I will forget and will resist. Playing Barbies isn't top of my interest list but making it a habit has helped me make it a priority. I need the ongoing reminder of my checklist and alarms to remind me to pursue my children in this way on an ongoing basis.

Identify the best time of day for you to have one-on-one connection time with your kids. If you have multiple kids, you may need to rotate how you do this time. The idea is for you to get a specific idea of how connection might be most easily incorporated in to your daily life.

Best Time of Day for You to Connect with Your Kids:

Step 2: Your Initial Daily Checklist

Having a printed-out, laminated checklist changed my life. Identifying habits that I want to adopt is easy, but implementing them into my life is a lot trickier. Having a checklist helped me to remember my habits and priorities and build confidence as I learned to incorporate them in to my life.

My Initial Daily Checklist

Self-Care	○ 7–8 hours of sleep (ideally lights out at 10 p.m., wake up by 6 a.m.)
	○ Gym workout for 30–60 minutes or walk the dogs around the neighborhood
	○ Spend 10–30 minutes reading and journaling in the morning
Daily 3	○ Make breakfast, prep lunch, and plan for dinner
	○ Unload/load dishwasher and clear off and wipe down kitchen counters
	○ Start one load of laundry and switch to the dryer
Stimulation and Fun	○ Create and post to Instagram *(progress toward area of challenge)*
	○ Deep work for 2–3 hours on book *(progress toward area of challenge)*
	○ Read a fun book for 30–60 minutes after school pickups before activities
Help Them	○ Hearty afternoon snack or early dinner so not hangry
	○ Get them exercise (playdate, go on a walk, practice, play in backyard)
	○ Connect one-on-one with at least one of my kids (ideally all three).

Here's what this initial checklist looked like for me. It will likely look different for you based on your daily three, self-care, and what stimulating things are most easily worked into your day. Through this chapter, I've helped you get some clarity on what habits you want to focus on to make progress in how you manage your ADHD and support your kids. Creating your initial checklist is where you learn to implement those things.

If you don't yet know your area of challenge, your stimulating activities will be more mini-hobby focused. There is immense value in your hobbies and interests even if you don't have a clear area of challenge to pursue.

You will notice that you will need to do some editing. You likely won't be able to fit every habit on to this initial list, and that is intentional. Let yourself focus on the specific habits that will help you the most initially. You will add more in time.

It's helpful to think about when you will incorporate these hobbies and habits into your life. Waiting until after your kids go to sleep to make time for stimulation and fun can really backfire. Learning to incorporate more stimulation and fun earlier in the day will give you the energy you need to make it through getting them to bed and will prevent you from staying up super late.

Trust me when I say that I understand that this initial checklist doesn't address all the things on your to do list. Mastering the fundamentals will give you the confidence and energy you need to add more to your plate. Let yourself focus on getting good at these things before adding more.

If it feels impossible, you need to edit your list to simplify the tasks and habits. The goal is to have a clear plan for making progress in the fundamentals. When completing your checklist feels consistently doable and you are able to complete the list 4-5 days a week, move on to the next step.

> **Step 2 Application:** Create your initial daily checklist using the checklist template available at https://www.amymariehann.com/mtmbook. Print and laminate your checklist and display it in an easy-to-see location. Begin checking off your items each day. Edit your list as many times as you need to achieve what feels like a right balance to ease the daily chaos. Completing your checklist should feel like a challenge but it shouldn't feel impossible. If it feels impossible, you probably need to edit your list. When completing your checklist feels consistently doable, move on to the next step.

5 | Master Your Daily Rhythm

The next step is for you to take the foundation you established in step 2 and give it an upgrade to create a little more structure to your days. Once you're able to consistently accomplish your list from step 2, you're ready to increase your personal expectations.

> *Consistently doesn't mean 100% perfect adherence! If you are completing your list four or five days a week, that counts as consistent enough in my book.*

The main goal in having a clear daily rhythm is starting your day with a clear plan for what needs your attention. When you go to bed, you know what time to set your alarm for because that doesn't change. When your feet hit the floor, you know what to do next because you've thought through your daily rhythm already. Fewer daily decisions mean you are burning less of your EF capacity.

Having this daily clarity means that you will spend less time "planning your days" and more time just living them out. And on low-energy days when it feels like your brain is barely functioning, you'll be less derailed because you have a blueprint to follow that doesn't require you to think or make decisions.

More Challenge and More Fun

You'll notice specific sections for both challenge and fun on the new daily checklist. This is really an expansion of what you did in the last step. Identify specific ongoing tasks and habits that you can work into your days so that you have the energy to do more taxing tasks.

If you are expecting yourself to do more taxing tasks, you also need to add more of the energy-giving activities that your interest-driven brain needs. So as you add more taxing tasks to get to the six or seven taxing-tasks threshold, you also will increase the stimulation and self-care that you are building into your days. You can't have one without the other.

Think of this self-care and stimulation as the fuel that will energize you to do the taxing tasks. As you get better at sprinkling self-care and stimulation throughout your days, you will have the mental and physical energy to maintain the six or seven taxing tasks on an ongoing basis without feeling depleted. In the following three chapters, I will help you unpack the weekly, monthly, and extra tasks, but adding more stimulation and self-care now will prepare you for those steps.

Morning Routine

Having a clear plan for your mornings is so helpful. The internet is full of complicated morning routines, and I'm sure that you have your own "ideal morning" list already. My advice to you is to focus on just three things that you want to incorporate in your morning routine. Decide what time you want to get up and then two morning self-care practices that you want to be part of your morning routine.

Downtime

Transitions are especially hard for those of us with ADHD. I don't know what it is but the pickup routine from school is always very draining for me and my children. I can remember so many times picking up my oldest child from school in the early years having planned a playdate right after school, thinking he'd be delighted, only to have him react with tears and exasperation. Where other kids might be ready to roll into an activity right after school, he wasn't, and honestly, I wasn't either.

I've realized that both my kids and I need a solid 20–30 minutes of downtime after pickups before moving into homework or leaving the house for an activity. They need a big cold glass of water or a smoothie, a good snack, and some time to recalibrate after school. And I need a little window to turn my brain off before moving on to afternoon activities and dinner prep.

For me, making afternoon downtime a part of my daily rhythm has been incredibly helpful. Without that time to rebound and transition from my workday to mom mode, I'm cranky and easily overstimulated. I often choose to take this time outside and leave my phone in another room so that I can have a short window to unwind away from screens.

Going back to the activation zone chart on page 25, we need margin in our lives to account for the unpredictable stressful things of life, like sickness, death, job loss, and other emergencies. If you don't have room for rest and downtime now, that's a clear indicator that you won't have margin when inevitable stressful things outside of your control happen.

As you go about your days, notice when you tend to get overstimulated and what circumstances surround the situation. Also, pay attention to what situations trigger your children and how an intentional period of downtime might help both you and they be better prepared. Consider how you might build a small period of downtime into your daily rhythm. After school might not be the right time, but identify what would work better for you.

This might look like:

- Reading, journaling, or listening to a meditation for 15 minutes before picking up the kids from school or daycare
- Listening to a 10-minute meditation while dinner is in the oven or while your kids watch a show after dinner
- Taking 20 minutes at the start of naptime to rest before starting a stimulating activity or taxing task

- Reading, journaling, or listening to a meditation during your child's music lesson or sports practice
- Having downtime from 12 to 2 p.m. on the weekends whenever possible to recover from sport games or birthday parties before starting an afternoon project, chore, or outing

Connection

Building authentic friendships where you feel safe to be yourself is hard to do when you are drowning in the daily tasks of life. If that's how you feel today, I promise that you won't always be in this place. But it's important to start thinking about your own need for connection on a daily and weekly basis. That will vary greatly depending on whether you are an introvert or an extrovert.

I value connection and need it, but I can easily get caught up with the daily tasks of life and forget about my friends and even getting meaningful one-on-one time with my spouse. I currently try and text one friend a day and I have that on my daily checklists because without that reminder, I will forget and find myself isolated and lonely. I'm honest enough with myself and the current limitations of this season of life to know that if connection isn't a regularly recurring thing on my calendar, it will likely not happen.

I encourage you to think about your personal needs in this area and how you might make meaningful connection a regular part of your life.

This might look like:

- Texting or calling a friend during car loop every day
- Calling a family member or friend during your commute
- Having recurring walking dates or coffee dates with specific friends
- Having a standing playdate at a certain park every Wednesday morning with a few favorite friends
- Planning a recurring monthly dinner out with a few girlfriends

Evening Routine

If it takes you a while to wind down for bed, you aren't alone. It takes me a solid two hours to wind down in the evenings even as someone who loves going to bed early. If I don't start my wind-down routines early enough,

I still won't be tired enough to go to sleep. I've had to accept this about myself and get intentional about how I prepare for bedtime.

One of the most common problems that I hear from moms with ADHD is the desire to go to bed earlier but struggling to make themselves go to bed. If this is a struggle for you, you aren't alone.

You aren't a robot that can be instantly reprogrammed to go to bed earlier. If your body, like mine, needs two hours to wind down and be ready for sleep, that won't change. Instead, you must focus intentionally on the wind-down effort. It doesn't need to be complicated. The simpler you keep it, the more likely you are to implement it.

Pick two evening habits that will signal the start of your wind-down period. When you start your wind-down period should correspond with the time that you identified on page 53 so that you give yourself enough time to be ready for bed.

I personally do my evening routines while my kids are taking their baths and sometimes even before they take their baths. As soon as dinner is done, I often take a hot bath, get in my pajamas, and then do my stretching routine. I am often still directing the kids through their evening habits *("Okay, now go brush your teeth")* while I'm getting ready for bed, but I am almost always fully ready for bed by the time I read bedtime stories to my daughter.

After I read to her, I usually climb right into bed and then read for another 30–60 minutes before I fall asleep. If I waited until my children were already asleep to start winding down, I'd go to bed much later. Having my own wind-down routine has helped my entire family to wind down.

My ADHD kids also need a good amount of time to get ready for bed. My bedtime routine is really our whole family bedtime routine. Maintaining this rhythm for myself also helps my kids prepare for bedtime and fall asleep more easily.

This might look like:

- Plug your phone in to charge in another room (not your bedroom) two hours before you want to fall asleep.
- Turn off all overhead lights and light candles.
- Take evening supplements.
- Make a cup of chamomile tea.

- Take a hot bath or shower.
- Play peaceful music.
- Complete skincare routine.
- Listen to a meditation.
- Perform a simple stretch routine.
- Use a massage gun.
- Do a relaxing mini-hobby like journaling, painting, coloring, or a puzzle.
- Read a fun book.

Step 3: Daily Rhythm

This next step is taking what you've learned so far about yourself and your needs for fun and stimulation and adding a little more structure to your days. You aren't trying to make yourself a robot or expecting every day to look the same, but you are creating an extra level of predictability to what you'd like your days to look like.

You get to decide how much structure you and your family need, so make this yours. If this feels too restricting and you need more flexibility, then do that. You'll identify the weekly, monthly and extra tasks in the upcoming steps so don't worry about those yet. But try and establish basic goals around sleep, self-care, stimulation, and fun. It's likely not much different from what you created in step 2, but having this added level of detail will make it easier for you to stay consistent.

Sample Daily Rhythm

Wake-Up	○ Up at 6:00 a.m.
	○ Prayer and journal time
	○ 45-minute weight workout at gym or jump on trampoline
Daily 3	○ Make breakfast, prep lunch, and plan for dinner
	○ Unload/load dishwasher, clear off and wipe down countertops
	○ Start one load of laundry and switch to the dryer

Challenge	○ Create and post a reel to Instagram
	○ Deep work for 1–3 hours
	○ Weekly task for my business
Self-Care	○ Walk dogs by myself for 30–45 minutes and listen to nonfiction book (goal of 10,000 steps/day)
	○ Make myself afternoon snack or smoothie at 3 p.m.
	○ Text or call a friend
Taxing Tasks	○ 2 weekly tasks
	○ 1 monthly tasks
	○ 1 extra
Fun/Novelty	○ Watch today show in the morning while doing daily three
	○ Read fun book for 20–30 minutes in the afternoon and after the kids go to bed.
	○ Watch a fun show while making dinner
Help Them	○ Hearty afternoon snack or early dinner so not hangry
	○ Get them exercise (playdate, go on a walk, practice, play in backyard)
	○ Connect one-on-one with at least one of my kids (ideally all 3)
Wind Down	○ Plug phone in at 8 p.m.
	○ Bath and stretching to wind down
	○ Lights out by 10 p.m.

Your daily rhythm should feel somewhat aspirational but be possible. This should include the habits you already adopted in step 2 with some new added expectations. You will likely struggle initially to build these habits into your life because change is hard, but they should be realistic—meaning that it's possible to do all these things on a normal day. It's okay if it takes you a few weeks to integrate these changes into your life, but if your expectations are unrealistic given your current constraints, scale back to identify a daily rhythm that feels more attainable.

Initially, I found it helpful to think about the natural flow of my day in how I lay out my daily rhythm so that I could use it as a guide throughout my days. I left my laminated copy on my kitchen counter so that I could refer to it throughout my days. But it's also important to remember that ADHD brains often crave spontaneity and it's okay if these habits and tasks don't happen at the exact same time every day. Following my daily rhythm got easier when I let go of rigid time frames and gave myself permission to go out of order and hop around as needed.

As you start using your daily rhythm checklist, remember that something is better than nothing. The goal in using these tools is more ongoing mental energy and to have calmer days. Completing any part of your daily rhythm will make your days less stressful and give you more mental energy. When you let go of needing to perfectly adhere to every aspect of your daily rhythm, it gets much easier to adhere to your daily rhythm.

> **Step 3 Application:** Create your initial daily checklist using the template provided at https://www.amymariehann.com/mtmbook. Print and laminate your checklist and display it in an easy-to-see location. Begin checking off your items each day. Edit your list as many times as you need to achieve what feels like a predictable yet flexible daily rhythm. Start implementing this daily rhythm and move on to the next step when you're completing your list 4-5 days out of the week.

6 | Master Your Weeks

For years, I struggled with cleaning my home. For me personally, tidying and organizing comes a lot easier but cleaning is something that I just really, really dread. And yet I also feel best when my home is both clean and tidy. I'm able to relax and my home feels so much more peaceful.

First, let me just say clearly that I have zero problems with outsourcing any aspect of managing my home and family life. If you have the means to do so, more power to you! I encourage you to outsource as many taxing tasks as your finances allow.

But when I found myself deep in ADHD burnout, we couldn't afford to outsource cleaning or yard work or much of anything. And I needed to figure out a system for managing the boring tasks of running our home that I could maintain.

Every single system that I found on Etsy or Pinterest or some mommy blog felt way, way too complicated. By that time, I had enough self-awareness to know that I needed a system that I could break up over the course of a week.

If I had any hope of maintaining this system, it needed to be a small list of right-sized tasks. These tasks should be big enough that they feel like a significant accomplishment but small enough that they feel doable.

But most importantly, I realized that I needed to shift my focus from always having a perfectly clean house to getting good at my predetermined list of weekly tasks. As I read parenting book after parenting book about raising kids with ADHD, the idea of praising effort versus results stuck with me, and I knew that I too needed to make that shift in how I was parenting myself.

I gave myself permission to let go of any externally based standards of what our home "should" look like and focused on what tasks help me and my family the most. I got as strategic as possible by identifying the 14 essential tasks that help us the most and allowed myself to get good at those before trying to take on anything more. This required me to prioritize and to let some things go, but it allowed me to get good at this pre-decided list.

As we dig into this next step of identifying your weekly tasks, it's imperative that you give yourself permission to find what works for *you*. You get to decide what calmer weeks look like to *you* and what habits and tasks best support you in that pursuit.

There isn't a right list of things that you *must* do to be a "good mom." You get to think outside the box and determine which tasks are most helpful to you on an ongoing basis. The goal here is to identify 14 weekly tasks that if you do these tasks most weeks, you will move out of that next level of chaos and have less ongoing stress.

You won't do these weekly tasks every single week. Let's assume you do these things 75% of the month. We are assuming that one week a month life will happen—you will get sick, your kids will get sick, a hurricane heads for your city, or some other energy-draining event. Or you may get hit hard when your cycle comes around and need to give yourself more rest that week. This expectation takes the pressure off. Initially, it helps to think about specific days for the different tasks to think realistically about your time on normal weeks. But that can also feel rigid and restrictive. I keep a laminated copy of my weekly tasks on my bulletin board on my kitchen wall. Each week, I check the things off as I go, and try to tackle two weekly tasks a day. Sometimes I do the things for that day but very often I skip around if that feels more interesting. Having that freedom and flexibility has allowed me to stick to this system for years.

This idea of having a list of weekly tasks may sound super obvious but it's so helpful for several reasons. Having a clear list of my expectations for myself means less time planning and making decisions, but it's been most helpful in building confidence. ADHD brains are terrible at letting us feel a sense of accomplishment. We always see what we haven't yet done and struggle seeing what we have done.

Your weekly tasks should cover the core tasks that you are expecting yourself to do on a weekly basis. If you do these tasks every week (or most weeks), your weeks will be much less stressful, and you will feel on top of the most urgent needs.

This process also helps you to prioritize your expectations of yourself and will very likely require you to do some simplifying to get your weekly expectations down to 14 tasks. You will need to ask yourself what you can live without or what you can delegate to someone else in your family to manage. Anything that requires your management and is on your mental load would still be one of your weekly tasks.

I've included three tasks (Mom Admin, Declutter One Thing, Deep-Clean One Thing) that I recommend and will explain in detail in the upcoming pages.

Possible Weekly Tasks

Mom Admin
Declutter One Thing
Deep-Clean One Thing
Fold the laundry
Put the laundry away
Wash all clothes (some prefer to do this weekly)
Wash towels
Clean or tidy bathrooms
Clean or tidy bedrooms
Clean or tidy family room
Vacuum and mop floors
Wash or change sheets
Update budget and spending tracking
Plan meals for the week
Meal prep
Order groceries
Water plants

Pick up groceries
Fill medicine boxes
Therapy or tutoring for one of the kids

Date night or one-on-one time with spouse
One-on-one time with a friend
Playdate
Therapy

Let me remind you again that there is no right list of weekly tasks. Only you can decide what is the most essential to you and your family. The important part is narrowing down your list so that you have clear and realistic expectations for yourself on an ongoing basis. The edit is the most important part because you won't be able to do everything that you want to do.

When you struggle with boring tasks and executive functioning, you must recognize and celebrate what you have done. Especially if you've spent most of your life trying to fit into neurotypical standards and beating yourself up for not making the cut, you must actively practice being proud of yourself. Positive reinforcement is much more effective than shaming and blaming.

In addition to my 14 weekly tasks, I also have two additional habits on my weekly checklist that are around relationships. I have added connect with a friend in person and connect with my husband. Those two habits are incredibly helpful to me, but I need that little weekly reminder to make those times of connection happen.

This weekly list is you proving to yourself week after week that you are showing up and doing the essential things to care for your home and family. I highly encourage you to print it out and laminate it and check it off with a dry erase marker. Each check-off will give you a little boost of dopamine.

Since 100% adherence isn't the goal, it's important that you don't try to play catch up if you miss a day. Moving down your list, you will miss a day sometimes, and that's okay. Work through your list, picking two each day, and when you've done all the things, wipe it clean and start again. Over time, you will get better at working through these things in a seven-day week.

Give yourself time to get good at these weekly tasks. In Chapter 13, I will share strategies and suggestions to make these weekly tasks easier. Once you are completing your weekly tasks most weeks, then move on to adding in the monthly tasks.

For example, you might currently go to the store every week to buy your groceries. The process around deciding what to buy, deciding when to go, going to the store, and then putting away the groceries is four different tasks. How can you make that fewer tasks? You might need to sign up for an online delivery service and figure out how to make that piece of your life easier so that you can meet that ongoing need in one task (order groceries) instead of four tasks. Give yourself the time you need to make those adjustments and solve those problems once and for all so that it's easier moving forward.

I don't meal plan weekly. I found that took too much mental energy, so instead I made that one of my monthly tasks. My meal rotation doesn't change much each month, so I've created a system that means I don't need to have meal planning take up one of my 14 tasks.

You get to decide what are the core 14 weekly tasks that are most important to you and that you want to plan to complete each week. You will have to let some things go and delegate some things to your spouse. You will also need to move some to your monthly list.

Pay attention to what tasks are the hardest for you and consider ways that you might make these easier for yourself. If you are struggling to complete the task consistently, it's probably too big or too small. The tasks should be big enough so that it feels like an accomplishment but small enough that you don't feel paralyzed to do it.

For tasks that are especially challenging for you, you may need to rely

> *"The decision fatigue and time blindness always made choosing what to do next impossible. I would either try to put too many things into not near enough time (in any reality) or just become mentally paralyzed and walk in circles. Once I decided what was actually important and deserved time in my week, I was able to make a decision-free list to work off of."*
> *MTM Community Member*

on body doubling (a productivity strategy in which the presence of another person improves your ability to focus). For example, I know that, left to my own devices, I will never look at our budget. It's my least favorite task, and I need the ongoing accountability from my husband in the form of a weekly coffee date to make that happen. I also need a weekly body doubling session with my membership community to update my business finances.

As you focus on getting good at your weekly tasks, you can identify what types of support, accountability, or accommodations you will need to make these weekly tasks easier for you. If you get stuck and need ideas, lean into AI and ask for tips to help simplify that area of your life. I'm a huge fan of ChatGPT and frequently ask for tips or suggestions when I'm stuck.

Mom Admin

One weekly task that I highly recommend is what I like to call Mom Admin, which you can retitle if you have something cleverer in mind. This is where I lump in the seasonal tasks around my home and family that are usually floating around my head, to help allay my fear that I might drop a ball of some kind. It's helped me to edit down this list each season and then to tackle one thing each week.

This one habit has helped me to stop overcommitting myself and to prioritize what matters to me. My Mom Admin list lives on my bulletin board, and I check off the boxes as I go. I have three different lists (Fall, Spring, and Summer) and try to keep each list to 15-20 things, which works out to roughly one Mom Admin task item a week.

I struggle the most with this list because I want to do all the things. I want to plan a big birthday party for each of my children and be the room mom for each class and host every major holiday for our extended family. Many of these things are fun for me—or at least fun in theory—but they also take executive functioning and planning. Having a clear list of Mom Admin tasks has helped me to pare down my expectations and to choose what I most want to give my energy to in this current season of life.

For me to stay within my six to seven tasks and live in my capacity, I had to prioritize what goes on my Mom Admin list and focus on what matters most. For example, I really like sending Christmas cards to our family and friends, but it does require a lot of executive functioning, and it takes up a lot of room on the list. Each year I reevaluate if that is still a priority or whether I'd rather say yes to something else like planning the kids' school holiday parties or hosting a Christmas party.

I like sending Christmas cards, but we don't like to travel at the holidays. If I tried to send Christmas cards *and* plan for our family to travel at the holidays, it would be way too much. I don't have the capacity to do both of those things during November and December. Your preferences and priorities may be different, so lean in to your own family's values and priorities.

Many of the things on these lists my husband can do, but these are the things that I want to do. I like picking out our outfits for our Christmas cards, so I don't want to hand that off to him. I know that if I can limit my focus to the things that matter the most to me, I'll have the capacity to show up and do them well. Editing my commitments in advance helps me to have the capacity to complete what matters most to me.

It's also helped me to realize that my capacity changes over time. For example, we are in our last season of recreation youth soccer, and I couldn't be more thrilled. My oldest has loved playing soccer but he will start high school next year and age out of the program. We will no longer be needing to remember snacks for soccer games and soon that spot on my Mom Admin task can be replaced by something else.

Here are my current three Mom Admin lists to inspire you as you create your own. There's no "right" list and yours may look very different from mine. I encourage you to let go of what you think "should" be on this list and focus on what you most want to prioritize.

Once you've done this exercise, print and post the Mom Admin list for the current season where you can see and work through it over the next couple of months. Tackling one Mom Admin task each week will help you avoid an immense amount of stress from last-minute scrambles.

My Current Mom Admin Lists

Mom Admin (Jan–April)	Mom Admin (May–Aug)	Mom Admin (Sept–Dec)
1. Register for Spring sports	1. Wash lunch boxes	1. Bring snacks to soccer
2. Get any needed winter clothes	2. Wash backpacks	2. Order Halloween costumes
3. Bring snacks to soccer	3. Finalize summer vacation plans	3. Get Halloween candy
4. Plan Frank's B-day	4. Pack for vacation	4. Get pumpkins
5. Execute Frank's B-day celebration	5. Unpack from vacation	5. Get Christmas card outfits
6. Frank annual physical	6. Clean out closet: Libby	6. Make Thanksgiving plans
7. Make plans for spring break	7. Clean out closet: Frank	7. Plan Libby's birthday
8. Plan Bowman's B-day	8. Clean out closet: Bowman	8. Update Christmas card list
9. Execute Bowman's B-day	9. Back-to-school shoes	9. Order Christmas cards
10. Make plans for Easter	10. Back-to-school clothes: Libby	10. Send Christmas cards
11. Clothes for Easter/spring	11. Back-to-school clothes: Frank	11. Execute Libby's birthday parties
12. Easter Baskets ×3	12. Back-to-school clothes: Bowman	12. Teacher Christmas presents
13. Research summer vacation plans	13. Print supply lists	13. Wish lists for kids
14. Book summer vacation	14. Get back-to-school supplies	14. Advent calendars
15. Research summer camps	15. Back-to-school night	15. Gifts for Mark
16. Book summer camps	16. Back-to-school forms	16. Gifts for grandparents
17. Teacher appreciation ×3	17. Labels for school supplies	17. Gifts for nieces and nephews
18. Spirit Days for Kids	18. Annual physical: Bowman	18. Get stocking stuffers
19. End-of-year awards	19. Annual physical: Libby	19. Plan meals for Christmas week and make any needed reservations
20. Get swimsuits, goggles, and sunblock	20. Register for fall sports	20. Make homemade gift for neighbors

Declutter One Thing

Every mom I work with mentions clutter as one of her biggest issues. There are many creators and entrepreneurs addressing clutter and minimalism as if solving this one problem is the key to unlocking all your issues around managing your home and family.

Clutter is a major struggle for many of us and can produce anxiety if it goes unchecked, but I have two major issues with this focus on clutter. The first is that this line of thinking assumes that once clutter is dealt with and you have solutions for your things, this problem goes away. But if you fundamentally struggle with organization, then dealing with clutter is an ongoing, lifelong thing. Second, I have just never personally been able to follow any of the declutter challenges. I would be gung-ho for a few weeks and then I'd inevitably lose steam and stop making progress.

The only solution that has worked for me in managing my clutter and organization is flexible, consistent action. One of my weekly tasks is to declutter one thing. When I first started this journey, I intentionally kept that goal very vague because it helped me keep making progress. Sometimes I would clean out a single drawer and other times it would be a whole closet. Though I usually did this on Saturdays, if I got a random burst of energy and wanted to clean out something on a Thursday night, I just went with it.

I initially focused on simplifying my areas and eliminating clutter. I wanted so badly to have clear rules for how many items to keep but what's worked the best is to just focus on keeping things I need, like, and have space to store. I didn't worry about any one space being perfect or keeping to any specific timeline. I just kept working through my home a little at a time and eventually worked through my home once and then twice and then a third time.

I now have very little clutter and see this process more as how I maintain my organization. After the initial purge, I next focused on function, and then on aesthetics. As I continue to work through my house decluttering and organizing a little bit each week, I now think about making it more aesthetically pleasing, as well as finding small tweaks to make our home function more effectively for us.

I still have my vague "declutter one thing" goal, which means sometimes I'm spending an hour and sometimes I'm spending 15 minutes on this process. Now my weekly "declutter one thing" looks more like me decluttering, organizing, or maintaining some part of my home. I have tried many times to create some kind of strategic schedule that I work through over time but that never seems to work. It's much easier to give myself flexibility and focusing instead on the ongoing habit of making time for organization.

Deep-Clean One Thing

Similar to my decluttering goal, for years I'd create elaborate cleaning schedules that addressed every area of my home but then I never seemed to do any of the tasks on the list and would feel like a failure. For me, tasks like cleaning my baseboards and dusting my bookshelves seem so daunting. I was great at creating the comprehensive strategy but not at implementing it.

Initially, I let these tasks go and focused instead on getting good at my weekly and monthly tasks. If that feels better to you, I encourage you to start there and maybe come back to this task down the road when you have more capacity.

Eventually, as I began to stay on top of my weekly and monthly tasks, I tried to add in deep-cleaning on a weekly basis and created another elaborate cleaning list of the more detailed tasks that I wanted to make myself do. And again, I neglected to complete any of these tasks.

I've now come to adopt a more flexible approach to deep-cleaning that works for me. I try to deep-clean one thing or one area of my house each week and let that be flexible. If I'm tidying my daughter's room and notice that her fan is dirty and decide to clean the fans at that precise moment in time, that counts as my one thing. If I open the oven and notice that it's looking gross and decide to run the self-clean cycle, that counts as my one thing. If I notice that my bedroom blinds are dusty and stumble on an Instagram reel about how to clean blinds, I roll with it and let that be my one thing.

This may sound chaotic, but taking the pressure off myself in this way and not feeling compelled to stick to a rigid schedule has meant that I'm much more likely to act, even if it's a little all over the place. Remember, the goal is to find a system that you can maintain, so if your system includes every detail of your house but you aren't completing those tasks, the system isn't working. Lean into what works for you and let go of arbitrary checklists that you can't implement.

Someone reading this is about to slip into a panic attack thinking, "But what if those tasks never get done?" So let me just be the one to remind you that they weren't getting done before! Putting them on the list doesn't mean they are more likely to get done. If those tasks aren't bothering you or your family daily, it's okay to just let them go undone and to decide they just aren't a priority right now.

You get to decide what "clean and tidy enough" is for you and you are allowed to let some things go as you work to create a system that you can maintain. In time, you may have more energy and capacity to tackle those deep-cleaning tasks. You may also decide that it's worth hiring a cleaner once or twice a year to do a deep-cleaning. But in the short term, you can choose to let some things go.

Step 4 Application: Create your Weekly Task List with your 14 weekly tasks and 2-3 additional relationship goals using the template provided at https://www.amymariehann.com/mtmbook or on a basic word document. Laminate this paper or put it in a laminated sleeve so that you can check it off as you go each week. Additionally, create your three Mom Admin lists with 20 tasks for each of the three seasons. Print the current season's lists and hang it in a place where you will frequently see it.

7 | Master Your Months

Now that your weeks are feeling less chaotic and you are on top of the basics, it's time to zoom out and think about how to inject more structure and predictability to your months.

This may sound easy but narrowing down your list of ongoing monthly tasks can be quite tricky if you are anything like me and there are far more than 21 things you expect yourself to get done in each month. It took me a while to get realistic about how much I could expect myself to get done in a month, which helped to reiterate how my executive functioning struggles impact my perception of time and my own capacity.

A huge part of why I felt like such a failure for so long was because my expectations for my time and energy were so out of whack. I'd look at people on the internet and assume that on any given weekend, I should have the time and energy to be able to host a party, complete a DIY project, spend two hours cleaning, and take my kids to do some fun outing.

I had to realize that the internet isn't real, so all of those little snippets of other people's lives doesn't mean that it is actually possible for anyone to do all of those things. But much more importantly, I had to learn that even if it is possible for other people to do all those things in any given week, it doesn't matter. All that matters is what I can do, and my own capacity and family's capacity may look very different from others.

> *All that matters is what I can do and my own capacity and family's capacity may look very different from others.*

I'll never forget this one busy October Saturday. My kids were 11, 7, and 3 and there was a neighborhood Halloween party going on down the street. It was your typical kid carnival-type deal with a DJ, bounce house, and all that jazz.

I can remember really, really not wanting to go and being so tired. We'd had a birthday party or something that morning, and I was already feeling depleted. The idea of small talk with random moms from the neighborhood and the sensory overload of 100 random kids running and screaming all hopped up on sugar sounded dreadful.

I felt like it was my duty to get them all in their Halloween outfits and show up so that my kids didn't miss any of the fun. We were all a little tired and cranky so it took a massive amount of effort to get us all there, but we made it, and I plastered on a smile for their sakes.

Well, about 20 minutes into the party, all three of my children came up to me and wanted to leave. It was too loud and too chaotic, and they weren't having any fun.

I had been so focused on proving that I could keep up with the other moms that I hadn't even considered whether the event itself would be too much for them. It turned out that the situation that I dreaded—the noise, the chaos, and the overstimulation—also deeply impacted them.

I incorrectly assumed that they "should" want to go to the Halloween party and have fun just as I was assuming that I "should" be able to push through and take them to the party. It was a major light bulb moment for me because I realized that I had to slow down and get a better grasp on what was best not just for me but for my kids as well.

I realized that skipping events or activities wasn't me depriving my kids but was actually me best supporting my kids, and that, as a family, we get to decide our main priorities.

I realized that skipping events or activities wasn't me depriving my kids but was actually me best supporting my kids and that, as a family, we get to decide our main priorities. I learned to let go of the "shoulds" and instead focus on finding a pace for life that works best for us.

I came to see that many of the things I assumed I could make time for weekly were more like monthly tasks. I had to learn to adjust my expectations around how many of these monthly tasks I could do on an ongoing basis.

This really helped me to have more realistic goals for myself and to focus on our core priorities as a family.

> *Side note: As I talk about monthly tasks, some of these things are more like activities. They might also be habits or events. You get to decide what makes this list.*

In a perfect world, I would have the energy on a Saturday to take my kids to the playground for four hours, then out to lunch, then do three hours of yard work before I painted one of the bedrooms and then hosted another family for dinner. All those activities might even fit into a calendar on one given day, but I know from experience that a day like that would completely deplete my executive functioning reserve.

Getting Realistic

Even if I wanted to do all those things and enjoyed each of them individually, collectively it would be way too much for me as an adult. It would also, I've reluctantly learned, be way too much for my neurodivergent kids. We'd all be cranky, overstimulated, and dysregulated.

Instead, I've learned to space out these expectations over the course of a month. I can make time for these individual things—a fun family outing, hosting friends in our home, yardwork, and tackling a home project—but I now think of these as monthly task items and realize that I need to sprinkle these throughout my month as opposed to cramming them in to one Saturday.

The key to identifying your monthly tasks is to think about three important things.

1. What are the core tasks that are most essential to your family that weigh on your mental load on an ongoing basis?
2. What are the core tasks/habits/activities that are most important to your family that you want to prioritize?
3. What can you realistically maintain?

I would caution you against adding a bunch of new tasks to your monthly list. For example, if you aren't currently in the habit of hosting people in your home at all and that would be a massive shift for you, maybe hold off on that. But if you are currently hosting your nearest and dearest for a BBQ every weekend and it's becoming a lot to manage, maybe shift that to your monthly list as something you want to continue but you need boundaries around.

I also encourage you to think about all the little random things that are part of your normal everyday life that float around your brain. For me that looks like returning library books, ordering refills of meds, picking up medicine at the pharmacy, dropping off donations to the resell shop, going to Costco, cleaning out my refrigerator, washing the dogs, and washing all the throw blankets. Getting all these random tasks out of your head and on to your monthly task list will free up mental energy.

One major struggle for many of us with ADHD is getting sidetracked. Since we struggle with memory, when we remember something that needs to be done, we feel the need to do it right away, then believe that we won't possibly remember the task in the future.

Having a clear plan for your monthly tasks really helps fight this urge. For example, when I take a quick work break to let the dogs out and walk past the basket with the throw blankets, instead of thinking, "I can't remember the last time I washed those. I better stop what I'm doing and put them in the washing machine," I know that I washed them last month and that I will get to them later as part of my ongoing plan.

I can still decide to wash the throw blankets right at that point, and if so, I'll walk over to my monthly task list and check it off. But I also know that I have a plan and don't have the same urgent need to address the issue right then if I'm in a writing flow and need to get back to work as soon as possible.

Identify Your Monthly Tasks

Going back to the goal of tackling six or seven boring things a day, my goal is to do one of these monthly tasks each day on normal and high-energy days. By limiting the list to 21 things, I'm planning for several low-energy days. On those low-energy days, I don't worry about accomplishing something on this list and I've built enough wiggle room into my plan that it's more realistic. Limiting your monthly task list to 21 things will require you to let some things go, but the editing process is a critical part of the process.

On days when I have the energy to accomplish something on my monthly list, I like to have the flexibility to choose. For example, I plan to do errands on Fridays, and I have a few monthly errands that I work through, but I don't expect myself to go through the car wash every second Friday of the month. That feels too rigid.

Limiting your monthly task list to 21 things will require you to let some things go, but the editing process is a critical part of the process.

Instead, I decide that day if I want to go through the car wash, return library books, or drop off my donations at Goodwill. I might even opt to do all three of those in one fell swoop if I have the energy and time that week. That flexibility is so important because if it gets too rigid, I will rebel and not do anything.

It's important that the tasks are very specific so that you can experience a sense of satisfaction when you accomplish them. Ambiguous tasks or tasks with many steps will feel harder to start.

I find that it's helpful to group my monthly tasks as I look at my weeks so that they make sense with my weekly tasks. Tasks that involve errands outside of the house I try to do on specific days. When I first started this method, I did try to stick to certain days because it helped me determine if my expectations were realistic. But now, just like with my weekly tasks, I give myself flexibility and often skip around with my list.

My Monthly Task List Broken Up by Day of the Week

PICK ONE MONTHLY TASK

SUNDAY	MONDAY	TUESDAY	WEDNESDAY	THURSDAY	FRIDAY	SATURDAY
Monthly Meal Prep	Monthly Budget	House Inventory	Plan Meals for the Month	Clean Out the Fridge	Costco /BJs	Fun Family Outing
Yard Work	Clear Out Paper Pile/Mail	Med Refills	Haircuts or Med Checks	Wash Throw Blankets	Wash + Vacuum Car	Home Project
Meal with Friends or Family	Home or Car Maintenance	Give Dogs Bath	Appointment for Myself	Ironing	Goodwill + Library	Date Night

As I've adapted this over time, it's been helpful to include in my monthly tasks things that aren't exactly tasks but more like intentional goals—like date night, a fun family outing, and even hospitality—which are fun but also take up energy. For a mom especially, even "fun" activities involve some sort of executive functioning and planning. I must remember the snacks, the sunscreen, the babysitter, etc., and all the remembering depletes my executive functioning.

Family Fun

It might sound like I'm suggesting that you stop having fun as a family, but that's not what I mean. However, there are a few normal ADHD tendencies that can make planning "fun things" for our family a little tricky:

- We tend to have all-or-nothing thinking and feel like we need to do *all* of the things right now.
- We are great at dreaming big and coming up with new fun ideas.
- We crave novelty and want to go try, see, taste, explore every new thing we learn about right away.

When my oldest was a baby and October rolled around, I remember wanting to go to the pumpkin patch and to go apple picking and to host a pumpkin-carving contest.

When December came, I wanted to host a cookie-decorating party and go see Santa and go to the Christmas parade and go to the downtown light festival.

When April came, I wanted to go to every Easter egg hunt possible and go pick strawberries and go on a vacation and host an Easter brunch.

Every time a new restaurant or park or local activity pops up on my Instagram feed, I send it to my husband because I want to go check it out "this weekend."

My natural tendency is to want to do all the fun things and pack our weekends full of activity. But as a mom with ADHD, married to a neurodivergent man and raising three kids with ADHD, I've had to learn to scale back my expectations and to focus on what activities are more important in this current season.

These big-scale fun activities require a lot of executive functioning for me. Remembering to pack the snacks, bring the sunscreen, find the parking, and all those little details add up. I must balance the extra "fun" with the extra capacity they will require of me.

Additionally, big-scale fun activities or outings can be overstimulating for me and my children and we often need downtime on weekends to recover from our normal pace of life. We have learned to be strategic about what we say yes too and have found that if we have the proper downtime we need, these family fun days are way more enjoyable. If we tried to pack our weekends with activities, my kids, my husband, and I would all be overstimulated and cranky.

I've realized that instead of trying to cram every activity in this year, I keep track of new experiences we want to pursue as a family and then intentionally try specific new activities each year. So if we want to go strawberry picking this April, we will opt to skip the Easter egg hunts. If we want to go to the Christmas parade, we will skip the light show.

Instead, we've leaned into smaller-scale, easier ways to have fun as a family on an ongoing basis. We love going on family walks. We love going to the movies. We love watching movies at home. We love going to our local park and the dog park. We love swimming in our pool.

Side note: I'd also lump travel in with family fun. If we are traveling as a family, that would count as our "family fun" for the month.

You ultimately get to decide your own capacity for "family fun" and you may have more of a need and capacity for large-scale

(continued)

> *(continued)*
>
> activities and outings than I do. What's important is knowing your needs and capacity.
>
> As I got honest with my own capacity, I often had a lot of mom guilt. I'd look at moms on Instagram who had the mental and physical energy for a big outing every weekend or for lots of family travel and feel like I was depriving my kids in some way. In time, I've come to think of this once-a-month family fun boundary as being not just about me but about my whole family. Honoring this boundary and refusing to overcommit and overextend out of insecurity that wasn't doing me or my kids any favors.

Over time, I've learned to better understand my capacity for home projects, hospitality, and doing fun activities as a family. I've come to see that even trying to accomplish these things once a month can be challenging for us. My entire family often loves a Saturday where we have no plans and can just be in our pajamas all day long. I used to have massive guilt for low-key rest days—what I like to think of "duvet days"—but now they are some of our happiest family days.

I've learned to temper my goals and have even gotten much more conservative about what I mean by "home project." In this current season of life, that often looks like hiring a painter or handyman to complete a project or making slow progress toward something over several months. Each month, little by little, we make some small progress in our home in a way that works for us.

Having a big picture of the month helps me avoid mom guilt. It's okay that we had a low-key Saturday at home doing house projects and watching movies. It's also okay if we took the kids to a theme park and had a blast but got nothing productive done. It all balances out over the course of the month, and I no longer expect myself to be able to check all the boxes each weekend.

Know Your Needs

Your capacity and your needs may be different from mine and that's okay. My little family is mostly made of homebody introverts who need a lot of time to recover after anything social.

Your family may be more social and thrive on being out and about with sports or community involvement. If that's the case, own those needs and let your monthly task list reflect your needs and priorities'. The goal here is to get honest about your needs and capacity and to clarify your expectations accordingly. Your list should be determined not by looking at me or at others around you but by considering your own needs and desires.

Pay attention to your family's natural rhythms. Do you also find that once a month everyone needs a down Saturday with no plans? If so, start planning for that! Instead of making social plans for every weekend, start blocking off one Saturday a month where you don't have plans.

Similarly, do you find yourself needing a spontaneous Saturday where you are out of the house doing fun things all day? Lean into that need and plan for a Saturday where you can be spontaneous. Listening to these natural rhythms and needs of you, your kids, and your family as a whole is so much easier than trying to fit these tendencies in week after week.

Boundaries

You may need to set some boundaries or to cut back in some areas in how you are currently living. If you are currently inhabiting the depletion zone and frequently dwelling in ADHD burnout, this is to be expected. You may need to step back from your current commitments and give yourself and your family more downtime.

You also very likely may need to lower your expectations in some areas. For example, for many years I tried to go through the car wash every week. I developed an ongoing habit of driving through the car wash every Wednesday and clearing out all the trash. But as my life got busier and my kids got older, that habit got harder. I looked at my weekly list and shifted that priority to my monthly list.

My car is far from ideal. I'd love to tell you that my choice to clean my car monthly meant that my family magically learned to keep the car tidy, but they haven't. My children could win gold medals in how to trash a minivan, and my car is very frequently what the kids might call a "dumpster fire." Nevertheless, I go through the car wash once a month, running the vacuum and wiping everything down. Even then it's still not perfect but it's "tidy enough" for me.

Over the course of the following month, it will get junked up again and depending on where we are in this whole cycle, if you open my car door at pick up, a wrapper, sock, or random shoe may very well fall out and bonk you on the foot. I've chosen to let this be okay and no longer stress or feel guilty about the state of my car. I've decided that once a month is what I can maintain and it's clean enough for my purposes.

I'm not a car person. I can't ever see myself buying a fancy luxury car or having a meticulously detailed vehicle. I'm more of a eating my Chik-fil-A sandwich as I drive, here are your chicken nuggets type, so I'm okay with this whole monthly cleaning the car thing. Of course, I've love it to be cleaner, but I accept that in this season of life, this is what I can maintain, and I know that I'm doing the best that I can to manage everything on my plate.

Do other people think my car is gross? Maybe, but I've decided to prioritize what works for me over meeting the arbitrary standards of others.

As you think about your monthly tasks, you will have to opt for less than ideal. But you get to decide what matters to you and what doesn't.

The goal isn't to find the perfect list where everything gets addressed. That won't happen. The goal is to have a plan for things that are more important to you and your family and to create a plan for staying on top of those things.

Practical Tips

I keep a laminated list of my monthly tasks on my command center next to the kitchen. Over the course of the month, I check things off it as I go. Sometimes I consistently pick one of the tasks for that given day, as I explain in the chart on page 97, but often it's more all over the place. It often helps me to pick whatever seems more interesting that day. The main goal is to have a clear idea of what monthly tasks are most helpful to you on an ongoing basis, and then to focus on getting those done before investing time and energy in other nonurgent tasks.

It took me a few months to edit my list of 21 monthly tasks so that it covered my biggest needs and desires for me and my family. Don't be surprised if you find yourself doing the same. Your list may differ significantly from mine, which is expected because we are different people. Give yourself the time to create an ongoing monthly list that reduces the chaos of your months by lowering the executive functioning required of you on an ongoing basis.

Having identified this list of monthly tasks and then learning to work through them consistently over time will mean less time spent remembering, planning, and prioritizing what needs to be done and create more capacity for you over time. Your months will be less chaotic, and you will be much more confident in your ability to stay on top of the things that matter most to you.

Step 5 Application: Create a monthly task list of 21 tasks, activities, or habits that address ongoing needs in your home and family using the template provided at https://www.amymariehann.com/mtm-book or on a basic word document. Don't expect yourself to remember this list of 21 things, because you won't, and having the clear visual will be a helpful reminder on an ongoing basis so that you can check things off as you go. Once you feel good about your monthly task list and are working through it each month, move on to step 7.

8 | Master the Extras

My brand of ADHD tends toward movement and commitment. I spent most of my 20s overcommitting myself and packing my schedule. I like saying yes and would rather be busy and on the go than staring at the boring tasks at home. It was easy to say yes to the fun things, but that led me to avoiding the boring tasks of adulting.

Looking back now, I see that much of my tendency to pack my schedule was a result of being underchallenged professionally. Planning parties, coffee dates, and adventures was a creative outlet for me because I was playing small in my work life. I needed that additional mental challenge, but it meant I left very little time to do the necessary tasks of life.

When I got married, this tendency got very complicated. My husband is also neurodivergent, though we didn't know that then, but he needs a lot more downtime. Where I wanted fun plans to look forward to every weekend, he craved white space and recovery time. We had many years of friction in this area of our life.

When I became a mom, my tendencies continued, and I would rather plan a fun outing than deal with the dishes. My oldest son, however, didn't do well with the constant activity. He craved stability, predictability, and alone time. I eventually realized that his behavior and mood were much better when we had a slower pace of life. He preferred going home after school over going to a visit a new park.

In time, I've come to see that I do much better when our lives are less busy. I still have a big need for novelty and stimulation, but I've learned that a frenetic pace of life and overflowing schedule isn't the most effective way to meet that need. My kids, my husband, and I are happier and more regulated when we have more white space and margin in our days.

And yet my brain is notoriously bad at visualizing my capacity. I tend to forget my commitments, and I've had to get creative at finding ways to help me understand what these extras look like in the big picture. Over time, I've found three things to help me end the overcommitting and overextending for good.

What Has Helped Me to End the Overcommitting

1. Trying to limit myself to no more one "extra" per day
2. Using a monthly calendar to visualize my extras
3. Planning recovery days as needed

Why We Overcommit

Though your reasons might look different from mine, overcommitting and overextending is intimately linked to how ADHD impacts our brains. Even if you know that it's a problem and you want to change, it can be hard to do so until you understand that this *isn't a character struggle* but is a manifestation of your ADHD struggles. Here are a few reasons why so many women with ADHD overcommit:

- **People-pleasing:** Making *other* people happy means a dopamine boost for our brain and we love dopamine. We often say yes before even considering our capacity or availability.
- **Working memory:** ADHD impacts our working memory, and we can easily forget other commitments and unintentionally double-book ourselves.
- **Lack of mental energy:** Sometimes we'll intentionally double-book ourselves knowing full well we can't do both things, but we just don't have the mental energy to troubleshoot the time conflict in the moment.
- **Need for novelty:** It's way more fun to say yes to the new random, exciting thing than to do our normal, repetitive, boring things of life. If you are in the boredom zone, your brain is seeking out what it needs.

- **Chaos is comfortable:** We are accustomed to a chaotic pace of life and find slowing down boring. If you've been living in the depletion zone and are stuck in fight-or-flight mode, this chaotic pace of life feels normal. You might not even know how to slow down the pace of your life.
- **Time blindness:** We genuinely think we can accomplish more than is humanly possible. We don't have a good grasp on time, but this isn't a character flaw—it's how our brains are wired. We need help understanding and visualizing our capacity.
- **Masking:** We are hyper-aware of what others are doing and feel obligated to keep up appearances that we are just as capable and able as they are. Saying no just doesn't feel like an option.

Learning to live in the activation zone requires that we get honest about our capacity around the extra things of life.

Limiting to One

As I've said over and over, I'm not here to tell you exactly how to live, but I am here to be your guide out of the chaos so that you can find a sustainable pace of life that feels good. Limiting my "extras" to one a day has been incredibly helpful to me and to so many in my community.

Remember, the overall goal is for us to get strategic about how many taxing tasks we are expecting ourselves to do on an ongoing basis. And the intention is for us to plan for a budget of six or seven taxing tasks a day. Well, the extra task is the floater that makes up that seventh taxing task.

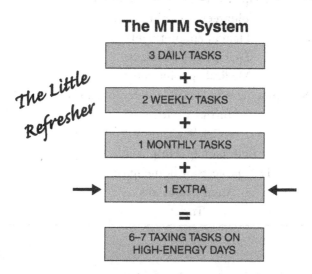

Our extras are those areas of life that take additional executive functioning but may not be weekly or monthly. Some extras (like kid's activities) are more predictable, but others seem more random.

Getting a handle on extras is essential in enabling us to live in our capacity. These areas of our life tend to be things we want to do, and without intentionality they can take up a good bit of our mental energy. Often these activities are fun for us or for our kids and can be life-giving, especially if you are an extrovert.

But these things also require planning, decision-making, and logistics. If you are the adult on duty at these events, it can mean remembering to bring a snack or change of clothes and then getting your kids out the door. Even if you are going by yourself, there is some amount of executive functioning involved.

You will likely want to think about "fun things" for your extras, but it is imperative to include those ongoing life maintenance things that you do on a regular basis, like appointments, haircuts, and errands. It's easy to forget about how those small tasks add to the ongoing mental load but they do add up, and planning for them will make a huge difference to your ongoing capacity. It also makes it exponentially easier to evaluate your capacity for adding something new to your life.

Examples of Extras

Kid activities
Therapy for you or your children
Volunteer commitments
Haircut appointments
Therapy appointments
Medical appointments
Shopping trips (especially Costco or Sams)
Birthday parties
Celebrations
Entertaining/Hospitality
DIY projects or home repairs
Attending events
Travel

Yes, I know that we discussed some of these things in the last chapter around your monthly list, but trust me on this. It will help your brain to understand your capacity if you can get a big-picture visual of what extras you have on the books for the coming month.

If our goal is to live within our EF capacity so that we aren't depleted and heading to burnout, it's imperative that we learn to limit the extras. I'm not saying that we eliminate them, but I've found that limiting my extras to one per day is incredibly helpful. Limiting my extras has also facilitated my kids getting the recovery time and downtime that they need on an ongoing basis.

OCTOBER 2024

SUN	MON	TUE	WED	THU	FRI	SAT
		1 ⚽	2 🎾	3 ⚽ 💃	4 Go to Costco	5 Soccer Game
6 Volunteer	7 🎾	8 ⚽	9 Haircuts for Kids	10 ⚽ 💃	11 Date Night	12 Soccer Game
13 Fall Festival Family Outing	14 🎾	15 ⚽	16 🎾	17 ⚽ 💃	18 Get Nails Done	19 Soccer Game
20 Volunteer	21 🎾	22 ⚽	23 🎾	24 ⚽ 💃	25 Painter's Come for Boys Bedroom	26 Soccer Game
27 Lunch w/ Grandparents	28 🎾	29 ⚽	30 Med Checks	31 TRICK OR TREAT		

This was a real month for me and my family. You can see on Thursdays that soccer and dance overlapped. They weren't at the same time, but they were on the same day. So my husband took my oldest son to soccer, and I took the youngest to dance. If my husband takes the kids, that doesn't count as my extra. He fully manages that ongoing commitment.

On afternoons where we have appointments (haircuts or med checks), we opt to skip tennis. I've learned that trying to do back-to-back activities is too much for me and for our kids. It's also helped me to identify that

Wednesday afternoon is always the best day for us to do appointments because the kids get out of school early. I try and schedule all medical appointments and haircuts for 3:30 p.m. on Wednesday afternoons.

I'm not going to say that we never do more than one extra a day, but I try not to plan for more than one. On a Saturday after my son's soccer game, if I have the energy to plan a last-minute playdate for my daughter or to take her to the playground, I do that. I've learned to expect myself to be tired and then, if I do end up having energy, to adjust accordingly. And as I've learned to do this and keep my plans light, I'm much more likely to have the energy to do more.

I also know that on the rare occasion that there is more than one major extra in a day, I need to try to simplify as much as I can. I've learned that, in order for me to stay out of the depletion zone, this needs to be the exception and not our normal way of doing life.

Having a Visual Calendar

I make a calendar like this on Canva for the whole year and fill in as much as I can initially and then update and print a fresh copy each month. I hang it on my command center next to my kitchen so that everyone can see what is happening. This calendar is my kid's favorite tool that I've created because they love to know what's coming and to be able to count down the days to certain things. My middle son crosses off each day with a marker.

Why would I do this, rather than buying a cheap calendar and filling it out? Well, I've purchased more calendars than I could ever count, and I'd never fill in the monthly things. It felt so cumbersome. Doing it on the computer and then copying and pasting recurring events is so much easier to me. Also, I have terrible handwriting that can be hard to read, and for some reason my brain just doesn't register things as easily that way. The same goes for any kind of dry-erase calendar.

My brain is very visual, and I need this tool to remember my plans. It's much easier for me to sit down and think through my life a few months at a time. Updating the calendar with graphics and different fonts so that commitments are easily differentiated helps me turn "updating the calendar" into more of a fun project.

As I think through our plans for each new season (Fall, Winter/Spring, and Summer), I update this visual calendar and use it to make decisions about my capacity. If I'm considering signing one of the kids up for a new activity or service, I consult this visual calendar, and it helps me to make decisions.

If you are going to go the traditional paper calendar route, I'd encourage you to get creative and find ways for events to stand out visually. For me, the exercise of sitting down to map out my extra commitments is an incredibly helpful habit. Over time, I've come to understand my own capacity and have stopped overcommitting and overextending myself.

As I mentioned, aiming for no more than one extra per day has been a helpful goal. My kids are currently 14, 10, and 6, which are very busy ages, but they're in school all day, so I have a welcome break. When they were younger and I was with them more of the day, my capacity was much lower, and we kept structured activities very minimal for as long as possible. Your capacity for extras may be less than once a day. The important part is knowing your capacity and then living within that as much as possible.

It's also important to think about your recurring appointments, shopping trips, travel, and home projects. Having this clear visual helped me to get realistic about my expectations for home projects. I now know that it's hard for us to make significant progress on any DIY project during the soccer season. After soccer games, we just don't have the energy and we need to outsource those projects, or prioritize them in the off season.

Thoughts on Therapy and Services

My children have been in therapies of many kinds over the years. We've benefited greatly from occupational therapy, play therapy, and tutoring in different seasons.

It can be incredibly overwhelming to meet all the needs of neurodivergent kids when it comes to therapies and services. Truly, it can feel like a full-time job driving kids from appointment to appointment.

(continued)

> *(continued)*
>
> Here's my hot take as someone who wants to help you end the chaos and overwhelm. Your well-being matters, and if you need to take a break from a particular service or therapy for a specific season, that's okay. That doesn't make you a bad mom. In fact, knowing your capacity and setting boundaries to protect your energy may very well better serve your children in the long term.
>
> I encourage you to talk to your children's physician and be honest. If you are limited in your capacity, ask them which services are the most important right now. What might you put on the back burner for the short term?
>
> I also find it helpful to have all ongoing appointments at a set time and day of the week. That will mean fewer details for you to remember and require less executive functioning. Additionally, if a provider can come to your home, opt for that. Eliminating transitions will make it easier for you and your children.

Recovery Days

The best way that I've learned not to let busy times of life derail me is to get intentional about recovery days after any big outing, event, or travel. I've also learned that outings and events are also really taxing for my kids, and they too need a down day to recover. Making this a normal part of how we do family life and keeping recovery days in mind as I put things on the calendar has helped us all avoid overstimulation and dysregulation.

After these types of events, I often have what I think of as an "executive function hangover." I'm tired physically but I'm also incredibly tired mentally and I need a low-key day to rebound before going back to my normal pace of life. On these recovery days, I keep my expectations for myself at a minimum and will likely only do my three daily tasks.

A recovery day for me means that I'm not going to plan any extra. We'll probably not leave the house, and I may even be in my pajamas the entire day. I will try to exercise or maybe go on a walk but if I need a full day under my duvet watching movies, that's completely acceptable too.

I find that if I give myself the day, I'm usually back to my normal energy by 3 or 4 p.m. and am then able to deal with any clutter or dishes and figure out something for dinner. We usually keep meals simple and may order takeout or bake a frozen pizza.

I might proactively schedule a camp or playdate for my higher-energy kids or ask my husband or mother-in-law to take them to the playground. But they might get a lot more screen time than normal on the recovery day and that's okay too. On those days, I'm not trying to win mom of the year. My goal is to be able to get back to my normal speed the next day instead of trying to push through my fatigue right away.

In general, being more mindful of how much executive functioning my daily life requires has helped me to develop more self-compassion around all that I do. It's helped me to take a moment to be proud of myself for handling all the details around the bigger things of life and to give myself that time to recover. Recovery days prevent me from getting depleted and act as a built-in margin when life gets more complicated.

Application

Start in your current season of life and think about the next two to three months. Map out your recurring commitments and include the extras that are your main priority. You may even want to reschedule or preschedule any needed appointments so that you can evenly spread out your extras. You may also need to take a break from some current commitments to simplify your life. Use this visual as a tool when you are considering new commitments for you and your family.

> **Step 6 Application:** Map out your extras for the next two to three months of your life on a calendar using clipart and eye-catching text, or markers and stickers. You can using the template provided at https://www.amymariehann.com/mtmbook or use my Canva templates available for purchase at www.amymariehann.com. Block off recovery days after any big events or travel. Make any necessary changes to your current schedule with the goal of one extra a day.

9 | Master Your Emotions

When I was deep in ADHD burnout, struggling with the huge emotions of my three neurodivergent kids and on an emotional roller coaster myself, it was not a pretty sight. My mood was all over the place and I'd get easily triggered by the whining, noise, and big emotions.

I kept seeing these Instagram videos telling me that I needed to be regulated to help my kids regulate their emotions, but I had no idea how to get there. I wasn't choosing to get triggered and I didn't want to be yelling at my kids, but I felt so stuck.

I was stuck in dysregulation. And yet, it felt impossible to get unstuck when I was drowning in the boring tasks of daily life. I didn't have the bandwidth to think deeply or to do the inner work of learning to process my emotions.

Regulating my emotions continues to be an ongoing journey and is at the root of everything I do to manage my ADHD. Getting adequate sleep, exercise, and nutrition all impact my emotional regulation significantly. As you incorporate and implement the strategies that I've already laid out in this book, you will make progress in your ability to navigate daily life and be less easily triggered by the events of your day and the big emotions of your children.

But much of the long-term change that I've experienced in this area of my life is the result of intentional effort around healing my nervous system. This required me getting in touch with my emotions and learning to identify and articulate my feelings. Years of ongoing therapy and personal reflection have been life-changing.

As you lower the daily chaos of your days, your weeks, and then your months, it's my hope that you will create space for you to go deeper in learning to manage your ADHD and regulate your emotions in response to daily life.

Though I can't attempt to address this complicated area in one chapter, I do want to offer some initial guidance as you learn to regulate your emotions. As you move out of burnout and have more capacity, I encourage you to focus on these five components:

1. Identify your regulated self from your dysregulated self.
2. Develop habits to promote regulation.
3. Develop habits for emotional release.
4. Focus on de-escalation with your children.
5. Focus on repair.

Understanding Emotional Regulation

My daughter and I recently stayed at a hotel for her cheerleading competition. My absolute favorite part of staying at a hotel is going to the pool. I'm a Florida girl through and through and I love time in the sunshine and in the water. And I love a good hot tub. There's something so regulating and calming to me about being in hot water. I take a bath almost every night and like the water to be just shy of scalding.

> Side note: If hot tubs make you think of Eddie Murphy and old SNL skits, we could definitely be friends. If you don't know what I'm talking about, please google "Eddie Murphy Hot Tub SNL" so that you can remember his voice saying "It's hot in the hot tub" from here on out.

This hot tub that we visited was pretty meh. It was more like a warm bath than a raging inferno, but as I got up to switch the little lever on the wall to turn on the bubbles, it got me thinking about emotional regulation.

You see, one of the hardest parts about emotional dysregulation is that even if we know that we are dysregulated, it's hard to find our way out. When we are deep in burnout and haven't learned to effectively manage our emotions, it's as if the little lever for the hot tub is broken.

Imagine that the water is our life and the little lever on the wall has two options: "dysregulated" and "regulated." Our broken lever is stuck on "dysregulated." The hot water is raging and we can't turn it off. And as great as a hot tub can be, it gets old fast.

So think about being forced to sit in an inferno-level hot tub past the point of comfort. How would you feel? Well, I for one would get irritated. I'd get cranky. I'd have trouble thinking and making decisions. Honestly, I'd probably be pretty bitchy to whomever had the pleasure of being in my vicinity.

If you are stuck in a state of dysregulation, it's no surprise that you'd be struggling. That you'd be cranky and irritable. That you'd have little patience for your children or your spouse. That you'd be easily overwhelmed and overstimulated. That you'd struggle with daily decisions. It's not because you are impatient or unkind or disorganized; it's because you are stuck in a less-than-ideal environment. It's because your nervous system is stuck in a dysregulated state.

The first step in learning to regulate our emotions is understanding that our lever is broken and to offer ourselves some kindness. And the second step is to understand that since your life is set to "dysregulated," you need to get intentional about seeking out regulating habits. To regulate your emotions, you need to climb out of the hot tub, walk over to the cold pool, and jump in for a refreshing dip.

In time, you can fix your lever by learning to heal your nervous system. A healed nervous system can experience moments of intense emotions (hot tub turned on) and then go back to a normal state of calm (hot tub turned off). This healing work is very important but it's also mentally draining and might be hard if you are currently in burnout. As you make more capacity in your life, you will create space (both time and emotional energy) to pursue this type of deeper healing work through therapy and/or ongoing personal growth.

But in the meantime, you need to prioritize climbing out of the hot tub. Each time you jump into the cold pool, you will return to your regulated self. The more frequently you do this, the more regulated, calm, present, attentive, and kind you will be for yourself and for your family. Walking over to the cold pool will be your lifeline until your lever is fixed.

Identifying Emotional Regulation

There are two main ways that dysregulation can look in those with ADHD. Some of us push our big emotions outward and are prone to drama, yelling, and rage. Others of us turn our big emotions inward and are prone to self-destructive behavior like overeating, overdrinking, or even impulsive spending. I'm of the latter camp and have spent most of my life suppressing my big emotions with self-sabotage.

My emotional dysregulation went under the radar and mostly looked like me sabotaging myself by making choices that were harmful to me. It didn't feel good and wasn't healthy. My dysregulated self was able to keep a facade of being kind and present, but I was constantly beating myself up internally.

Once I became a mom, this often looked like very negative self-talk around the state of my home. I'd see dishes in the sink and feel like the worst mother in the world. The overwhelm wasn't as much about the dishes as it was the critical thoughts in my head. My self-sabotage based on my emotional dysregulation made the tasks feel so much bigger and harder and more daunting.

Though rage or anger isn't my go-to, my dysregulated self does often get very irritable and easily annoyed. I am impatient and am constantly on the move. I get very easily overstimulated and am very easily distracted. It's hard for me to stop and think intentionally about my actions and instead I'm driven by an my internal motor constantly reacting to whatever feels most urgent in that moment.

I encourage you to think about what your dysregulated self is like and how that version of you differs from who you really are when you feel most content, calm, and yourself. You might even want to give your dysregulated self a name. When you feel that self taking over, take ownership of that and then consider what you might need to send her packing her bags.

Promoting Regulation

So what does it look like practically to jump into a cold, refreshing pool to regulate your emotions? I don't pretend to be a PhD in emotional regulation so this list isn't comprehensive, but I'm sharing here what has been most helpful and easily applicable to my life as a busy mom of three young kids.

The big changemaker for me was understanding that I needed to proactively incorporate these habits into my everyday life and not just use them to deal with acute emotional dysregulation. Can these strategies help you to calm down when you do get fully dysregulated? Yes! But if you can learn to get out of the pool *before* you are all hot, bothered, and irritated, you will avoid the worst of your dysregulation symptoms.

As you get better at identifying when you are feeling slightly dysregulated and make these habits regular parts of your life, you will be able to endure the heat for a few minutes because you will know how to jump right out and cool down when you need it. Your life will be an ongoing circuit of heating up in the hot tub, followed by a cool dip, and then repeat.

But to get there you must first make these habits a part of your daily life.

Breathwork. I honestly hate that term. It sounds so new-agey, hippy-dippy, and frankly complicated to me. But intentionally slowing down your breath is incredibly effective at calming your nervous system so that you can return to a state of regulation.

I am all about keeping it simple, which is why I love box breathing. I breathe in for five seconds, hold for five seconds, breathe out for five seconds, hold for five seconds, and then repeat. There are many other breathwork strategies, but this is the one I prefer because it's the easiest for me to remember.

I intentionally do this type of breathing every morning while I drink my tea and then every evening before bed. Before bed I either stretch or lie with my legs up the wall. Setting aside just five minutes at the beginning and end of the day to slow down and breathe has been a helpful in healing my nervous system.

You may prefer to use a different breathwork exercise, follow a guided meditation, or even do a slow yoga routine. Find what feels best to you and what you can consistently incorporate in your daily life to proactively reset your nervous system.

Polyvagal eye roll. I won't attempt to unpack the polyvagal theory (created by Stephen Porges) here, but having a basic understanding has been incredibly helpful. My very novice explanation is that there is a pathway between the hot tub and the cold pool and by engaging the vagus nerve we can shorten that pathway.

Many of us are stuck in the hot tub because our pathway is blocked. We know that we need to get into the cold pool but we can't see how to get there, so we stay stuck, hot, and irritated. It's as if a large shrub has blocked the pathway and we need help clearing the pathway so we can get to the cold pool. Intentionally engaging the vagus nerve works to clear the path so that we can easily move back and forth between the hot tub and the cold pool.

By shortening the pathway, we then make it easier for ourselves to move from the hot tub to the cold pool when needed. So when we get dysregulated, we can quickly get back to regulation. In time, this is what works to heal our nervous system because we're no longer stuck in dysregulation. Instead, we eventually can jump back and forth easily from the hot tub to the cold pool.

As I have tried to wrap my brain around the polyvagal theory and implement it in my life, this basic exercise from Dr. Stanley Rosenberg in his book *Accessing the Healing Power of the Vagus Nerve* has been incredibly helpful to me. I do this exercise each evening after I stretch or while I have my legs up the wall.

The Basic Exercise from Dr. Stanley Rosenberg

Step 1: Lying comfortably on your back, weave the fingers of one hand together with the finders of the other hand.

Step 2: Put your hands behind your head, with the weight of your head resting comfortably on your interwoven fingers.

Step 3: Keeping your head in place, look to the right, moving only your eyes, as far as you comfortably can. Do not turn your head; just move your eyes. Keep looking to the right.

Step 4: After a short period of time—up to 30 or even 60 seconds—you will swallow, yawn, or sigh. This is a sign of relaxation in your autonomic nervous system.

Step 5: Bring your eyes back to looking straight ahead.

Step 6: Leave your hands in place, and keep your head still. This time, move your eyes to the left.

Step 7: Hold your eyes there until you notice a sigh, a yawn, or a swallow.

You don't need to be an expert in polyvagal theory to benefit from this simple exercise. There are a plethora of YouTube videos and blog articles demonstrating this exercise, so check out one of those if you want a more detailed tutorial.

As you seek to better understand the polyvagal theory, I encourage you to explore the works of Dr. Stephen Porges, Dr. Stanley Rosenberg, and Deb Dana. I personally have found the books by Deb Dana to be the most easily accessible.

Grounding. Grounding is really coming back into our body and finding moments of calm and safety throughout our days. Grounding can be done with anything that engages our five senses. It also works to calm our nervous system.

This might look like:

- Cuddling with a weighted blanket on your lap while you read or watch a show
- Butterfly tapping
- Gentle movement like stretching
- Giving yourself a hug or asking for a hug from a family member
- Holding something that feels good to you
- Cuddling and petting a dog or cat
- Lighting a favorite candle or making a yummy-smelling cup of tea
- Dancing, throwing a ball, or even stomping your feet

Grounding in nature, called earthing, might also be helpful. It's thought that when our bodies come in to direct contact with the earth, it neutralizes positive ions in our bodies, which calms our nervous system.

This might look like:

- Taking breaks from holding your phone or even having it near you
- Spending time outside and feeling the light of the sun
- Walking barefoot on the grass
- Sitting or lying down on the ground outside
- Spending time gardening

Somatic music. One of the easiest ways that I've found to regulate my nervous system is by listening to somatic music. Somatic music can regulate your emotions by triggering your parasympathetic nervous system.

Types of Somatic Music

- Slow-tempo music
- Classical music
- 432 Hz frequency
- Nature sounds
- Binaural beats

There are many different options for somatic music, so find one go-to playlist that helps you to relax. Then identify a few times during the day when you might listen to this playlist proactively.

I found a playlist by simply searching "somatic music" on my music provider, Apple Music. I like listening to my somatic playlist if I'm sitting in a sauna at the gym, while stretching in the evening, or even while going for a walk. When I find myself getting easily dysregulated or feeling more stressed, I try to proactively listen to this playlist more frequently.

Emotional Release

I spoke about emotional release in Chapter 4, but I'll reiterate it here. Intense exercise, verbally processing with a friend or therapist, journaling, a creative hobby, and dancing to music are all healthy emotional outlets to help you release your pent-up emotional energy. These things also provide space for you to process your actions and behaviors and to reflect on why a certain situation may have led you to get dysregulated.

When I was deep in ADHD burnout, I was also lonely but didn't have the energy to pursue friendships. As you create more space in your life, that will change, and you will have more capacity to invest in meaningful friendships that can support you in this way.

Regardless, you still need some ongoing meaningful way to proactively process and release your emotions so that they don't derail you. Hard exercise is incredibly helpful to me, but I have also greatly benefited from ongoing talk therapy. It can be difficult to find a counselor or therapist who understands ADHD, but finding the right fit can be life-changing.

I've found that having a therapist who has ADHD themselves is very helpful. It's often difficult for me to process and package my thoughts and feelings, and what I need most is a safe space where I can just kind of vomit it all out in a stream of consciousness. It's in that process that I'm able to identify my thoughts and feelings. I have felt better understood and safe to share openly with therapists who themselves have ADHD. I've felt safer to share openly and authentically.

De-escalation

Part of our foster parent journey required us to take classes in trauma-informed parenting and it was truly life-changing. Trauma-informed parenting goes against many modern parenting practices and discipline strategies. And as a parent who had read all the mainstream parenting books and found them falling flat, this approach really resonated with me.

It was like a light bulb went off and I knew that this strategy would work better for my kids when they were having big emotions and tantrums. The traditional methods of threats, time outs, and expecting compliance never worked to calm them down and always left us both feeling crappy.

Way before I understood what it looked like to regulate my own emotions, de-escalation was a helpful first strategy in learning to manage my own dysregulation and help my kids when they got dysregulated. It gave me actionable steps to take in the heated moments of daily life.

De-escalation isn't terribly complicated. Think of your raging kiddo as an out-of-control fire. More fire (raised voices, critical words, or threats) just make the fire grow bigger. Instead, our children need a big bucket full of water thrown on them to extinguish the fire and bring their energy back to normal.

In those hard moments of big emotions, our focus needs to be on de-escalating the big emotions by being calm and level-headed. Initially, this was a huge challenge. Their big emotions were very triggering for me and my natural impulse was to meet my fired-up kids with more fire, and that never helped.

But when I understood the assignment, I got better at learning to stay calm myself and then learning to de-escalate things when my children got fired up. I also learned how I could de-escalate things for myself when I got fired up.

I wanted to know how to respond when I lose my cool or when my kids lose their cool, but even more importantly I wanted to learn to avoid that as much as possible. I started paying a lot more attention to when we're overwhelmed and working to make modifications so that we don't lose our cool. I practice these things for myself and talk about them with my kids daily.

Going back to the hot tub analogy, when my kids are overheated and stuck in the hot water, they don't need me to climb in with them and get overheated. They also don't need me to try to fix the broken lever in that moment. They need me to gently guide them out of the hot tub into the cool pool so that they can get back to a regulated state.

Living in a neurodivergent family where everyone struggles with emotional regulation can be such an emotional roller coaster. As I've processed my own ADHD struggles, one of my main recurring negative beliefs is that "I'm too much." As a parent, I so badly want my kids to feel safe, to articulate their emotions, and to feel free to be fully themselves. And yet, if I'm honest, some days raising three neurodivergent kids feels like too much to me—the emotions, the noise, the needs. I needed a way to navigate their big emotions and needs without passing on the shame that I experienced.

> *I've come to realize that navigating emotions in a neurodivergent family is a two-way street.*

I've come to realize that navigating emotions in a neurodivergent family is a two-way street. Sometimes my kids are incredibly loud and emotional and volatile. And sometimes I'm incredibly emotional and reactive and sensitive. We want to point fingers and assign blame to the other party but for our family to thrive, we all need to learn to navigate our emotions and show grace and kindness to each other.

I don't have this whole thing mastered, and I lose my cool far more than I like. But I'm also incredibly proud of the progress that we've made as a family and the emotional awareness that my kids have. My husband and I are constantly amazed by the tools that they have, even as we feel so imperfect in our ability to love them well. This awareness didn't come from hanging up a cute sign on my fridge about emotions but from actively living this out and applying this understanding in our day-to-day lives.

The most effective thing we can do to help our kids regulate their emotions is to prioritize our own emotional regulation and to model for them the ongoing regulating habits. We'll be better able to de-escalate their big emotions and have the bandwidth to avoid being triggered by their big emotions.

My daughter is currently six years old, and our biggest struggle right now is helping her to navigate her overwhelm without lashing out with unkind words. It's hard in these moments for me to navigate de-escalating her big emotions without addressing the mean words she's projecting at me, her brothers, or her friends.

After these episodes, she's been able to tell me that she uses the mean words when she's overwhelmed and tired. We've been talking through other things she might say or do when she's overwhelmed to let us know that she needs a break or doesn't want to talk.

Last night, my husband was feeling all sorts of tired and overwhelmed. He had just gotten home from sitting in a noisy gymnasium for an hour, followed by a 30-minute drive, and he was trying to navigate making a cup of tea while also talking to our daughter about something. I attempted to give him an update on something, and he just didn't have the capacity to listen right then.

I honestly don't even remember the exact words that he said to me, but he kindly told me that he was overwhelmed and tired and asked if we could talk about it later. There was no malice or anger in his tone, and I was glad to give him the space that he needed. As someone who has been on the receiving end of this same kind of grace and understanding, I was glad to give it to him. My feelings weren't hurt, and I didn't take his need personally.

I immediately turned to Libby and said, "Honey, did you just see what Daddy did? He was overwhelmed and tired and he told me so without using any mean or unkind words!"

I could honestly tell you hundreds of stories like this one of how this plays out in our family life daily. This is taught day in and day out as we do family life together. We still lose our cool, but we've learned to de-escalate when needed, to model habits that we can use when that happens, and to encourage everyone in our family to support each other along the way.

This might look like:

- Observing how certain habits impact our kid's moods. "You are in such a great mood after playing on the playground and spending time in the sunshine!"
- Remaining calm when our kids are dysregulated and waiting until they calm down to talk about it.
- Actively pursuing your own regulating habits and owning it when you are dysregulated.
- Communicating our own needs openly to our kids on an ongoing basis.
- Listening to our kids when they let us know they are overwhelmed and need downtime. This includes not pushing them in to activities or events when they've expressed this need.

Repair

Emotional dysregulation is inevitable. It's futile to expect yourself never to get overstimulated, overwhelmed, or dysregulated. As we get better at managing our own ADHD and setting boundaries around our time and energy, these times will get fewer, but they will still happen. We need to be prepared for what to do when dysregulation impacts our daily life.

Dysregulation can look many ways but it's usually some mix of big emotions or angry words that we don't mean directed at the people we love the most. When you lose your temper with your children or spouse, it's crucial that you know how to repair the relational damage. If you lean in to repairing things with your loved ones, these episodes can lead to healthier relationships and a deeper emotional connection.

Our kids don't need us to be perfect. They need us to show them how to navigate relationships and emotions in a healthy way. They need to see us owning our challenges, and they need to know it's okay for them to do the same. They need us to model repairing with them on an ongoing basis.

How to Repair with Your Loved Ones

- *Pause and reflect:* Take a moment to calm down and reflect on what happened before approaching your child. You may need to give it a few hours.
- *Acknowledge your behavior and ask for forgiveness:* Use clear and simple language to take responsibility for your behavior and to clearly state that they didn't deserve that treatment and did nothing wrong. For example: "I am so sorry that I yelled at you. You don't deserve to be spoken to with that tone and that didn't reflect how I feel about you. You didn't do anything wrong and I was out of line in my reaction. Will you please forgive me?"
- *Validate their feelings:* Show your child that their feelings matter. For example: "I imagine that felt scary and overwhelming when Mommy yelled like that. I'm so sorry that I made you feel that way."
- *Explain without excuses:* You can briefly explain why you were upset but be careful not to shift blame to someone else. For example: "I didn't sleep well last night and I'm tired and a little cranky today. I got overwhelmed by all of the noises. It wasn't fair of me to take it out on you."
- *Make a plan for next time:* Show them that you are committed to doing better and brainstorm about how to handle the situation in the future. For example: "Next time I'm feeling overwhelmed, I'm going to walk away and go in my room until I can calm down."
- *Reconnect with love:* End the repair with some gesture of love like a hug or kind word. If possible, do an activity together or cuddle and read a book.

I wish I could say that I never lose my temper or say or do things that I regret with my family. But if that was the case, my kids would never hear me acknowledge my own mistakes and ask for their forgiveness. And without a doubt, the single best thing that I've done as a parent is teach my children this skill. When they come to me on their own after acting out and acknowledge their behavior and ask for forgiveness, it makes my heart swell with pride. It's a beautiful thing and a gift to them and their future relationships.

My parents didn't have this training or these skills, and it's one of the reasons why I spent so many years trying to be perfect. I was so afraid to make mistakes and to admit to any weaknesses. Teaching our children to repair is actively teaching them that it's okay to be imperfect and that owning our struggles leads to greater intimacy.

Emotional dysregulation will occur, but you get to decide if it will damage your relationships with your children or strengthen them.

Exercise: Self Reflection
- Describe your dysregulated self and give her a name.
- Identify one new regulating habit that you want to incorporate into your daily life.
- Identify your one or two go-to outlets for emotional release.
- Create a go-to script that you can use to repair with your loved ones.

10 | Master Your Energy

When I left my corporate job to become a stay-at-home mom, I thought that my challenges in managing my home life would get easier because I mistakenly thought more time would mean that I could get more done. But the reality is that more time is very rarely the solution to the problem, especially when it comes to completing mundane tasks.

Most traditional self-improvement books focus on time management as the means to master productivity and to accomplish more. But those strategies are often not effective if you have ADHD. All tasks are not created equal to our brains and if we don't fundamentally understand that, we'll never learn to make our brains do the boring things we tend to avoid.

ADHD brains fundamentally struggle with motivation, especially when the tasks are boring. We may want to complete a task and have the time to complete a task but if the task itself is dull, our brains don't produce enough motivation to get us to do the task. Having more time doesn't make us more likely to do the task. In fact, our brains will likely wait until the last possible moment and rely on urgency as the motivator to get the task done. Our brains will often go rogue and find something random to accomplish instead of using the extra time to do the task we need to do.

Don't get me wrong. I'm a busy mom and struggle getting all the things done just like you do. More time always sounds appealing, but learning to manage your energy is an essential step in learning to master the mundane things of life as a woman with ADHD. If you don't first figure out the energy piece, more time will never result in getting more of the essential things done because you will still find a way to procrastinate or waste your energy on nonurgent tasks.

Our ability to hyperfocus is an absolute gift, and it means that how we use time and energy can look very different from others. We may be able to hyperfocus on an interesting project for six hours and accomplish more than someone else can do in a 40-hour work week. At the same time, completing a 15-minute task may illicit such dread and anxiety that it's harder for us than those six hours of interesting work. What matters isn't the amount of time but the energy required from us to do the specific task. Doing more boring tasks requires learning not how to get more time but how to get more energy. And more specifically, learning to understand how much energy we have and how we can best allocate our energy to meet the demands of our life.

ADHD brains literally hate doing unpleasant tasks. Boring tasks feel painful to us. Avoiding them is not us choosing to be lazy but it's a natural involuntary reaction. It's almost like a self-preservation tool. We really and truly *want* to have accomplished the task and aren't choosing to procrastinate; it's like our brain prevents us from doing it.

We can learn to do the boring things of life, but doing so consistently over time requires that we learn to charge our batteries, allocate our energy, get honest about our energy tendencies, and learn to navigate low-energy days.

Charging Your Battery

I've already extensively covered what it looks like to manage ADHD well. These same strategies are your tools for charging your battery. This isn't an all-or-nothing thing. Your battery may not always get fully charged and there will be seasons where you have more time or less time for the habits that help you. But having a clear understanding of what habits are the most helpful to you and what you can intentionally pursue in this current season of your life will enable you to get the energy that you need.

If you are struggling to do the taxing tasks of life, you are probably depleted and need charging. Designing a life where you proactively get the charging you need before you are depleted is essential. Over time, as you make more time and energy for the things that energize you, you will have more capacity for the boring things of life.

I fully understand that this may sound counterintuitive. How can spending more time and energy doing fun things make someone more productive? But so much about what works for the ADHD brain is counterintuitive to traditional productivity coaching.

CHARGING YOUR BATTERY

Self-Care
- Sleep
- Nutrition
- Exercise
- Emotional Regulation

Stimulation
- Challenge
- Novelty/Fun
- Connection

Rest
- Intentional EF
- Low-Energy Days
- Recovery Days

It might feel like a leap of faith to invest more energy in charging your battery, but consider how exhausting the burnout cycle can be for you and your family. When you are depleted and living beyond your capacity on an ongoing basis, it's basically like you're stuck in a place of dysregulation and incapable of thinking clearly and making progress in the boring things of life. I've already discussed how this place of dysregulation is often accompanied by intense feelings of self-judgment. As a result, the pretty normal response is to want to take action through massive change. We have a strong instinct to overcompensate for these bad feelings by blowing up our lives.

One member of my membership community so aptly called it "big black bag energy," where we want to go gangbusters on the clutter and chaos. But big black bag energy is just another form of dysregulation. And this big, bold change made in haste is its own unique type of exhausting. Though we've taken bold action, we are still depleted, and since we were reactive, nothing sticks. We may appear to be more "productive" but it doesn't make our lives any less chaotic in the long term. It doesn't move us forward toward our goals, and it wastes a lot of energy.

When people tell me that they've tried everything, I wonder how much of that trying has been during times of big black bag energy. I know I've been guilty of that. But those changes never stick.

Instead, we're better served by focusing first on charging our batteries, getting back to regulation, building up our reserve so that we can focus on creating a sustainable plan for allocating our energy, and tackling the mundane things of life. As we create simple systems and routines that we can maintain, we create capacity for more boring things over time. This is exactly the process that I've been leading you through in this book but it's important that you really understand how important this energy piece is to being able to make these systems stick. If you aren't making time for your interests, for novelty, and for challenge, your efforts so far will all be in vain and the MTM system will be just one more thing to add to your collection of failings.

Allocating Your Energy

A lot of things are fighting for your mental and physical energy. How do you manage your energy well so that you don't end up depleted again?

I've come to understand that I need to allocate my energy to three core areas of my life: intentionally completing the priority taxing tasks, intentionally pursing my big ideas, and intentionally supporting my neurodivergent kids. This does not mean that I allocate time evenly among these three areas, but it means that I had to recognize that to be the kind of mom I want to be, I must intentionally give these three things priority in how I'm using my energy. Embracing all three also meant that I had to get clear on my personal expectations in each of these areas of my life.

ALLOCATING YOUR ENERGY

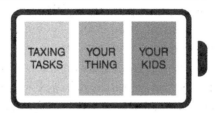

You see, for many years I vacillated between a few extremes when it came to how I was allocating my energy. As I've already mentioned, I've always been a perfectionist by nature and expected myself to be the best at every area of my life. So I tended to go all in on perfecting one area of my life while neglecting other areas in the process.

As I've worked with others, it's become clear that I'm not alone in this. I've identified four clear tendencies when it comes to how we allocate our energy and how that can impact our quality of life and our daily stress level. I've been stuck in all these tendencies in different seasons of life.

As you read through these, try to identify what tendencies you most relate to now and which you think you've gravitated to in the past. Consider how these tendencies might be at the root of the challenges you identified in Chapter 2.

THE FOUR TENDENCIES

Tendency One: Unrealistic Perfectionist

Tendency One is what I like to think of as the *Unrealistic Perfectionist*. This is the woman who has unrealistically high expectations for her home and for her ADHD brain. She has a long to-do list of boring things that she expects herself to blow through. She's not making time for anything that is stimulating or interesting or for real meaningful self-care. She's aiming for a Martha Stewart level of the perfect ideal and has created numerous iterations of complicated systems, trying to facilitate a way to check all the boxes.

As a result, her brain goes rogue daily. She finds herself easily sidetracked by random nonurgent projects. She is busy all day but when the end of the day comes, the important tasks of daily life still didn't get done. She feels like a failure for not being more "productive" because she didn't do the things that she really needed to get done, but she also didn't do anything fun or energizing.

She's an expert at what I like to call "pro-crastivity," which is basically nonstop activity while still managing to neglect the boring basic things of life. Her brain gravitates to the tasks that feel more fun and interesting even though they aren't a priority.

Basic Things of Life

By basic things of life I mean those tasks that are necessary for daily life. These tasks get very boring because they are monotonous and repetitive.

- Having a plan for meals
- Performing basic work tasks
- Having food to eat
- Having clean clothes to wear
- Have a safe and clean place to live
- Fulfilling basic hygiene habits
- Getting enough sleep
- Getting to school or work on time
- Arranging transportation to and from school and activities for children
- Supporting children in meeting their academic requirements

This tendency may be partially impacted by perfectionism. If she feels incapable of doing the task perfectly, she will delay doing it and choose something more accessible. This can also be a self-fulfilling prophecy because if she uses the same rationale not to pursue challenge, she stays stuck and bored. She is tired but unfulfilled and her daily life still feels very stressful despite her effort.

The longer this lasts, the more this internal tape of shame and self-sabotage gets reinforced. As you drop balls daily, you believe you may be incapable of change. You feel like you don't deserve to do anything for yourself until you can get your life together.

If this describes you, despite what some might think, you are not consciously trying to rebel, which feels even more frustrating. You want to get the taxing tasks done but can't make yourself do them. You are exhausted but your daily life is still very stressful because the necessary, important tasks keep falling through the cracks. It's defeating and embarrassing. And you don't have the mental energy left at the end of the day to navigate the normal challenges of raising neurodivergent children, which is triggering and leads to more dysregulation for you and your entire family.

If you identify with Tendency One, you must learn to prioritize charging your battery and reserve energy daily for the big needs of your family.

Suggestions for Unrealistic Perfectionists

- Identify a mental challenge to pursue on an ongoing basis.
- Inject fun into your life through mini-hobbies, pursuing interests and meaningful connection.
- Build downtime into your days so that you have the energy needed to support your kids.
- Lean into the MTM framework, starting with step 1, identifying your daily three. Give yourself time to work through the steps.
- Change your internal dialogue to become your own biggest cheerleader when you do boring things.

Tendency Two: Overwhelmed Overthinker

Tendency Two is what I like to think of as the *Overwhelmed Overthinker*. This woman started out as an Unrealistic Perfectionist but is too stuck to take any action. She is great at creating the long list of all the things that need to be done but then is too overwhelmed to take any action. She knows what needs to be done but can't seem to make herself do it despite her best efforts.

She has lots of guilt for being so stuck and doesn't feel like she deserves to do anything energizing or stimulating until she's gotten herself unstuck. She might watch a few hours of Netflix or spend time doomscrolling but that's not restful or restorative—more of a coping mechanism and procrastination tactic.

She ends up relying on urgency to get the basic things of life done at the very last minute, which is also stressful for her entire family. She feels like she should be able to make herself be more productive and better use her time but at the root it's an energy issue. She didn't get anything done but she also feels weirdly drained from being stuck in paralysis.

If this is you, you're likely making two big mistakes. First, you are not doing enough to charge your batteries in the first place, which is leaving you depleted. Second, you are spending what little energy you have creating your daily unrealistic to-do list. You need to learn to charge your battery *and* to conserve your mental energy by having a simpler system that you can execute without wasting energy on planning and prioritizing.

If you start the day without a clear plan, it takes a massive amount of energy to get you in motion. For those who struggle with prioritization and decision paralysis, this is a recipe for disaster. You are basically setting yourself up to fail. Having a predetermined, simple routine that is realistic enough to get you in motion will help you avoid the paralysis trap.

Suggestions for Overwhelmed Overthinkers

- Lean into the MTM framework starting with step 1, identifying your daily three. Give yourself as much time as you need on each step even if you need several months at each step.
- Rely heavily on visual tools to give yourself a clear plan of what needs your attention so that you can avoid overwhelm and paralysis.
- Inject fun into your life to reward your brain for doing the basic things of life.
- Find what you are naturally good at and truly enjoy, and look for ways to bring more of that into your daily life.

Tendency Three: Passionate Procrastinator

Tendency Three is what I like to call the ***Passionate Procrastinator***. This woman knows her strengths and has found a vocation or creative outlet that lights her up. She enjoys what she does and is good at it.

She shines at work where she feels capable but struggles with the boring tasks at home. So it makes total sense why she'd give most of her energy to work and tend to procrastinate dealing with the basic things of life and the boring tasks at home. Her interest-driven brain is choosing what comes more naturally and is more enjoyable.

She's come to find over the years that if she waits long enough, her old friend urgency will kick into gear and give her the energy she needs in the nick of time. But the downside of urgency is that though it can help us pull through at the last minute, it's very draining and stressful. Urgency is one strategy to move ADHD brains into action, but it's best reserved for emergency situations.

If you rely on urgency to accomplish the basic daily functions of life on a regular basis (such as waiting until the last minute to create a plan for dinner or panic-washing the laundry), this creates an enormous amount of stress for you and your family. It's hard on your kids and on your marriage. Urgency is better reserved for things like doing your taxes or family emergencies.

It's important for us to know our strengths and to actively pursue challenge, but we must do so with boundaries. Our brains will always want to prioritize our passions over the boring mundane things, but we have to create realistic expectations based on our executive functioning challenges and to learn strategies beyond just urgency for getting our brains to do unpleasant things.

What I unexpectedly found is that when I got better at creating boundaries around my work, the quality of my work, the clarity around my ideas, and my creativity improved exponentially. It turns out that the stress of relying on urgency takes an enormous toll. Additionally, feeling like a failure in one area of life leaves us feeling like an imposter and hinders our progress and success in other areas too.

> *When I got better at creating boundaries around my work, the quality of my work, the clarity around my ideas, and my creativity improved exponentially.*

I'm going to ask you to trust me on this. As you start creating boundaries around your passions to make more time for fun, self-care, and addressing the basic things of life, your stress level will lower and improve every area of your life. Chaos is not in your long-term best interest.

Additionally, as hard as it is to accept for many of us, neurodivergent kids have big needs. We must make space in our lives to help them charge their batteries too. If you are regularly dealing with dysregulated kids and behavior challenges, you know exactly what I'm talking about. As you learn to lower the stress around the daily things of life, you must also intentionally create space for caring well for your children and getting them the support they need before they get dysregulated.

I was forced into making major changes around my work life after I hit my massive ADHD wall. I had been building a business from home in the nooks and crannies of my life for over eight years. I was in nonstop hustle mode, hoping that I'd eventually earn enough to be able to outsource all the boring things I hated. In the meantime, I was neglecting and ignoring those things as much as I could. It wasn't a winning strategy for my business or my family. The boring things didn't get done, which created stress and chaos and my business was stagnant.

I pulled away from that first business and realized that how I was living was unsustainable. I needed a plan for managing my home and family that worked for my current financial circumstances, and I needed to create very clear boundaries about when I was working and what I was trying to accomplish each day and each week. I focused my energy on one big challenge at a time instead of trying to pursue every idea at once. I also focused my energy on creating automation to accommodate my ADHD tendencies.

I don't share these things flippantly as if you live in a dream world where these changes have no ramifications. Financially, it was incredibly difficult initially, and we cut way back in many areas, believing that it would pay off. Over the last several years, this intentional change led to massive change for our family and for my business. I am working much less, earning much more, and am more creatively fulfilled and inspired than I have ever been.

My husband also made several job changes over the last five years to find a role that provides him the right work-life balance. He's currently working 100% remotely, which he's found to be the right fit for him and for our family.

I'm in no way stating that you should blow up your life, shelve your big ideas, or give up on your dreams. I'm not contradicting what I've already shared about the importance of challenge and mental stimulation. But you must learn to pursue your goals in a way that makes room for the self-care that you need while also meeting the big needs of your neurodivergent kids.

This doesn't mean you are capable of less but that your life may need to look different. You may need to slow your pace for a season as you learn to effectively manage your ADHD and create systems for managing your home and family life. In doing so, you will create more capacity and be more effective, successful, and productive in your career and creative endeavors over the long haul.

Suggestions for Passionate Procrastinators

- Put some challenges or ideas on the back burner for the time being.
- Lean into the MTM framework starting with step 1, identifying your daily three. Give yourself time to work through the steps to create systems that work for you and your family.
- Break down your current challenges into realistic benchmarks that you can achieve over time and celebrate your progress along the way.
- If possible, move to a four-day work week, or to working remotely partially or entirely.
- Hire a virtual assistant for the more mundane aspects of your professional life.
- Hire an ADHD coach to help you create better habits for managing your professional life so that you can complete your tasks in less time.
- Create weekly professional goals so that you have a feeling of completion and know when you can be "off duty."
- Automate as much of your professional life as possible.
- Prioritize exercise, sleep, and downtime as necessary parts of your creative process.

Tendency Four: Professional Parent

Tendency Four is what I call the *Professional Parent.* This is the woman who is extremely focused on supporting the big needs of her neurodivergent children to the detriment of her own well-being. Every book she reads, podcast she listens to, or course she buys is about caring for her children and learning new ways to support them.

She feels overwhelmed by trying to learn everything. She may be homeschooling her children as well and is also likely trying to navigate multiple therapy appointments each week. She doesn't get any time to herself and feels guilty spending time, money, or energy on her own interests.

If she does anything creative, it's somehow for her family's benefit. She's planning a birthday party or working on their home in a way to serve her children. Caring for the needs of her neurodivergent family has become her identity, and she's lost touch with what she likes and enjoys doing for herself.

She knows she should be prioritizing self-care, but her needs are at the bottom of the list, and they never seem to take priority. As a result, she's depleted because her battery is never getting charged and her daily life as a caretaker is incredibly draining. Though she loves her kids immensely and wants to be able to support them, she often struggles to regulate her own emotions and to implement the things she's learning. She is working so hard to be a great mom but feels like a failure.

But here's the hard truth. Your neurodivergent kids will learn more from the lifestyle that you model for them than anything you will ever say. Learning to manage your own ADHD and to charge your own battery on a consistent basis so that you can do the mundane things of life is the most effective thing you can do for them. Additionally, you can't help them regulate their emotions if you aren't regulated. Your well-being directly impacts theirs.

> *Your neurodivergent kids will learn more from the lifestyle that you model for them than anything you will ever say.*

I'm in no way advocating abandoning all this intentional parenting and learning. Instead, I'm encouraging you to let go of the need to figure it *all* out right now and to prioritize both charging your battery *and* learning to support their needs. Doing so is the only way to truly be effective in implementing new things that you learn so that you can best support your kids in the long run.

We must embrace the belief that it's okay to be an imperfect parent and to be learning these things as you go. Parenting neurodivergent kids while also reparenting yourself and learning to manage your own ADHD struggles is hard. You can't and won't learn all the things right away.

It's unrealistic to expect yourself to figure it all out right away. Give yourself permission to be a work in progress. Doing so will give you the freedom to focus intentionally on pursuing behavior change in one or two areas at a time, which will increase the likelihood that you'll be able to successfully implement a new parenting strategy or tool. It will also give you energy to care well for yourself.

Suggestions for Professional Parents

- Take a break from homeschooling (or seek out more support) because you need some time to yourself to charge your battery.
- Address one area or concern in your children's life at a time and allow other areas to get a pass for the time being.
- Lean into the MTM framework starting with step 1, identifying your daily three and prioritizing your self-care habits.
- Make time for your own interests and inject fun in small ways throughout your days.
- Pursue some kind of ongoing support like a therapist or parent coach so that you have the support you need if you are in the trenches of navigating difficult behavior challenges.
- Establish a set weekly time when you can get time away from your home to pursue an interest or challenge.

Navigating Low-Energy Days

One of the hardest things about living with ADHD is the energy fluctuation. Sometimes, despite my best intentions and efforts, my energy is low. For women, this is especially common at the end of our cycles. The several days before our periods start and then the first few days of our cycles can be especially challenging. The decrease in estrogen impacts our dopamine, which in turn impacts our brain's ability to function.

Additionally, once we understand what goes into charging our batteries, it makes sense that when we don't sleep well, or miss a workout, or cancel our therapy session because of sick kids, we'd be depleted and lower in energy. This often happens to parents, despite our best efforts.

> *You make every effort to get to bed early and fall asleep by 10 p.m., only for a toddler to crawl in your bed and kick you in the groin all night long, leaving you exhausted the next day.*
>
> *You lay out your workout clothes and set your alarm to get up at 6 a.m. so you can go for a walk before your kids' wake up, but at 5:30 your son gets a stomach bug and is puking all over you.*
>
> *Your spouse is going to cover dinner and the bedtime hours so you can go write at a coffee shop for a few hours, but then he has a work emergency and you are stuck at home making mac and cheese for the fifth night in a row.*

Even when you learn to charge your batteries and shift your expectations, life is going to happen and you won't always be able to get your battery full charged. In those cases, we need to recognize and adapt to low-energy days.

> **Low-Energy Days**
>
> *These are the times when you have lower mental, physical, or emotional energy than normal and need to adjust your expectations of yourself accordingly.*

I've found it incredibly helpful to do a simple check-in with myself in the mornings:

- How is my energy? Is it normal, low, or high?
- How did I sleep? Am I rested or tired?
- How are my emotions? Are they normal or intense?

It's almost like a choose-your-own adventure story. If I have low energy, didn't sleep, and am feeling very on edge with my emotions, then all signs are pointing to that being a low-energy day. I then try and mentally adjust my expectations. I accept that my energy is lower and don't try to push through to get all my weekly

"The idea of budgeting my energy was a game changer. I had not thought of my energy as a thing to manage or even consider; I only ever considered the mountain of work looming ahead. Whether

> *I had budgeted energy seemed inconsequential. Wow, was I wrong. Once I did the time blocking and the daily three, weekly, monthly, and mom admin lists, my mountain was now chopped up into smaller hills. I also changed my thought process around the energy-boosting things as being a reward only. They were no longer things I only got when the mountain was climbed (because that was never going to happen); now they were what was going to get me up the mountain. I didn't have to feel guilty for resting anymore. I knew I could get the things done because I had a system that worked for my brain and energy needs."*
>
> *MTM Community Member*

and monthly tasks done. On low-energy days, I focus on completing my three daily tasks and getting the rest and self-care that I need. I let a lot of things go and focus on rebounding. I don't try and play catch up on the next day.

Instead, I've embraced the idea that low-energy days are a very normal part of living life with ADHD. Allowing myself to adjust these expectations has meant that low-energy days don't derail me or deplete me. I also have much fewer low-energy days because I now know how to charge my battery on an ongoing basis.

Additionally, it's incredibly important that you don't take the low-energy day to mean that you have done something wrong or that you are a failure. A very common tendency is to respond to low-energy days with big black bag energy, assuming that since your energy is low, your systems must not be working and need to be replaced with something new. Trying to reinvent the wheel is a huge waste of energy, and this tendency is very much a signal of dysregulation and a lack of self-trust.

My intentional plan for my executive functioning has left room for low-energy days. I don't plan for perfect adherence and give myself permission to do less if needed. This has meant that when I need to take a duvet day, I allow myself to do that, and I don't beat myself up about it. I'm then able to get back to my normal routines quickly because I have a clear plan for managing the boring things of life.

I don't try to make up for the tasks that I missed and I focus on moving forward. With my weekly tasks, I focus on just getting back to two weekly tasks in the future and don't try to do the tasks that I missed. If I try to play catch-up every time I have a down day, that feels very overwhelming. Allowing myself this flexibility has meant much fewer down days overall.

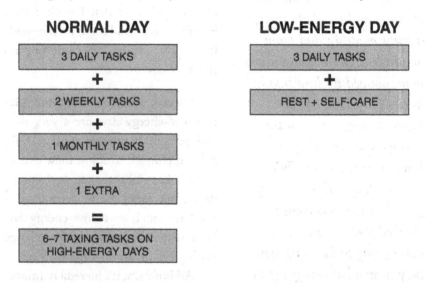

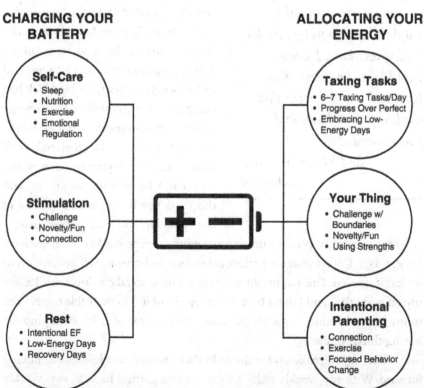

Your Energy Plan

The biggest barrier for most of us is the idea of what our life "should" look like and what we "should" be able to accomplish in each day, week, or month. But the reality is there is no right way to do life as a mom. The goal of this process is for you to get clear on your own capacity and to be honest about the needs of your brain, your family, and your children so that you can start living within your own capacity and living to your full potential.

Living this way requires you to let go of pursuing perfection in any one area of your life. You won't have the perfect home or be the perfect parent and you won't be able to pursue every big idea that you have right now. But by letting go of perfection, you will be able to make significant growth in every areas of life.

> ### Exercise: Self-Reflection
> - What is your energy tendency?
> - What are one or two of the suggestions that you want to try to implement in your life?
> - What ways will you intentionally pursue charging your battery?
> - Where are you currently allocating too much of your energy?
> - What areas of your life need you to allocate more of your intentional energy?

11

Automate Your Life

Once I got clear on my weekly and monthly priorities, I focused on how I could streamline and simplify those things so that they took less time and energy.

I was a child of the '80s, so automation always reminds of watching the *Jetsons* cartoon show and all the fancy gadgets they had to make their daily life easier. Or maybe even Cher's closet in *Clueless*. I wanted that fancy closet.

But the automation strategies that help me the most are pretty low tech. I think of automation as making decisions once to limit ongoing choices and decisions. My goal in automation is to reduce the number of variables and changes to my daily life.

I have slowly created different strategies around different areas of my life and then tried to create infrastructure to implement those strategies. Left to my own devices, I will forget any plans or intentions and need to plan for that tendency.

For example, I may decide that my kids are going to get one hour of iPad time after school but the next day when they come to me with puppy dog eyes wanting more time to watch dumb YouTube videos, I will completely forget. I know that living this out needs to be super easy for future me, so when I make the decision around the screentime limits, I update the kids' screentime limits on their iPad so that they are automatically limited to one hour of access Monday through Fridays from 3:00 to 8:00 p.m. Now future me doesn't have to think about whether or not they should get more time.

Okay, maybe that was a bad example because that is pretty techy. The best way to explain my approach to automation in my home and family is that I totally hyperfocus and problem-solve one area of my life and then work to make it as easy as possible for future me to implement. I assume that future me will forget and need visual reminders.

The tendency to hyperfocus on a specific problem is incredibly common for moms with ADHD so you are probably nodding your head to that, but the infrastructure part might be new. Through self-awareness, I now accept that I will always forget what I decided and for it to really make my life easier for future me, I need to create some way of remembering. That often looks like a printed-out checklist, but sometimes it's as simple as a labeled note on my phone that I can easily pull back up. It often looks like setting up recurring reminders or alarms or leaning into electronic resources.

It's helped me to think about one area of my life at a time and to make it my project. I love projects and it feels like a challenge. I don't aim for perfection but instead focus on specific change that I can implement. I then try and create infrastructure to help me implement that in the future.

One common fear that I hear from my community is "*What if it gets boring?*" but I've learned to assume that it will get boring and that over time I will need to tweak each strategy. But I don't let this fear stop me from creating some kind of automation strategy. Instead, I create a plan for now, and then I come back and tweak that strategy over time as needed.

It's also important to mention that I stopped trying to get my novelty/stimulation fix from these little home projects. If I'm mentally bored, it's very tempting to want to reinvent the wheel and come up with a new meal plan, cleaning schedule, decluttering plan, and so on. This is exactly what I mean when I talk about "big black bag energy" because you're seeing the project and problem as a means of stimulation and novelty. Once it gets boring, you no longer want to stick to that system. But if you are seeking out novelty and stimulation in other areas, it's much easier to stick to systems over time.

Initially when I was focused on creating systems for my home, I found focusing on creating change or automation in one area of life per month to be realistic. Now, I revisit all my systems with each new season and tweak things as needed. I invested a lot of initial energy and have no interest in starting from scratch in any of these areas. Instead, I just make small tweaks and changes to keep things interesting. Don't try to find the perfect solution but focus on a small change or tweak that makes your life easier, and give yourself room to continue to make tweaks to improve that area over time.

Automation Examples

- **Meal planning:** Print out your favorite 10–15 recipes and put them in a binder in your kitchen. Create a "meal options" list of your go-to recipes to make meal planning easier and hang it on your fridge. You can also ask ChatGPT to create this list if you have specific preferences or dietary constraints.
- **Shopping:** Create an inventory list of your normal purchases. Print it out and use it to know what you need to buy each week or each month. Create recurring automatic orders for those things you buy consistently.
- **Money/bills:** Set up all bills on auto-pay and create a simple spreadsheet of ongoing expenses.
- **Birthdays:** Create a list of all important family birthdays. Put all dates on your calendar with a one-week reminder to purchase a gift or send a card and to send a text to that person.
- **Screentime:** Create a screentime contract and set up automatic parameters on all relevant devices.
- **Communication:** Create email folders and set up filters so that your email is automatically sorted and you don't miss important messages.
- **Travel:** Create a packing checklist for any frequent trips and print it out to use repeatedly. Ask ChatGPT to create this for you if you need help.
- **Smart home automations:** Program things in your home using timers and apps wherever possible. Smart vacuums, dishwashers, lights, alarms, and washing machines often have features that you can program to go off automatically.

As you find solutions that work for you and your family that you can implement on an ongoing basis, you will create more capacity over time. Creating automation doesn't have to be complicated to make your life easier.

> **Automation Application:** Pick one area of your life where you'd like to create automation. Spend one hour thinking through how to make this area easier and creating some kind of infrastructure to make it stick. Templates for the automation exampled provided are inluded in the Tools + Templates pack available for purchase at www.amymariehann.com.

Your Weekly Flow

Creating a weekly flow might not seem like it's a form of automation, but for me it's been the ultimate automation move. I struggled for many years with creating structure for our days that worked for me and my family. I tried so many tools and strategies and found this one strategy to be incredibly helpful in wrapping my brain around our life and commitments.

Do you know what I mean by wrap your brain around something? It's the best way I can explain how my brain works. I really struggle with conceptualizing information, especially dates and times and commitments. It was one of the reasons that I struggled with overcommitting for so long. I just didn't have a good gauge on all the commitments that were coming at me and didn't understand the capacity piece of it. My ADHD brain just saw the request or obligation as "fun" or "not fun." If it sounded fun, I wanted to say yes even if I didn't have the capacity.

My brain needs help understanding my capacity and visualizing that capacity on an ongoing basis. I needed a clear plan for my life, but sitting down to map out my schedule every day or every week is incredibly unrealistic. It burns a lot of EFs, and I need a clear plan that I can fall back on during low-energy days or when I'm struggling to think clearly about my capacity and everything feels overwhelming.

I needed predictability and structure, but I also needed it to be flexible enough not to feel restrictive. The fewer moving pieces there are in my life, the less EF my daily life requires. And yet I realized that it's unrealistic for all my days to look the same because that gets boring really quickly. I needed a clear, repeatable plan for my weeks that required fewer decisions and provided my family with the predictability we needed.

More than anything, I needed to spend some time each season mapping out my capacity so that when requests came, I would have a clear sense of my capacity to add anything more to my plate. The weekly flow isn't as much about rigidity to specific time frames but pre-deciding the flow for your weeks at the outset of each new season so that you can better make decisions.

I started creating this tool for my family each season basically as a rough plan for our weeks. The fewer variables there are in our weeks, the better off I am. I created ours on Canva and I update it in May (for summer), in August (before the new school year), and in January (at the start of the new year).

Some people might look at my weekly flow and think, "You are so organized!" and that is not what is going on here. I've learned that I need to fill this out so that my life makes sense to me. The actual exercise of thinking through the logistics, making ongoing plans for that season of life, and creating a visual representation is necessary for my brain to understand my ongoing commitments and constraints. Some people may easily be able to picture how all these commitments play off each other, but I must sit down and map it all out for it to sink in as I'm planning out my life.

Accepting and embracing this fundamental need and making time to think through my commitments has helped immensely. I've also come to realize that I really struggle to think clearly and to make decisions when I'm in mom mode. It's easier for me to think through our weekly flow for the next several months at a coffee shop by myself with little distraction than it is for me to navigate small decisions of daily life each day in the presence of my children.

Additionally, I've realized that my brain functions best when there are few variations from week to week. It's easier for me to remember that our med check appointments are always on Wednesdays right after school. It's also easier for my kids because they know exactly what to expect on those days. Each deviation from the norm requires more executive functioning (remembering, reminding, adjusting, decision-making) so finding an ongoing routine that is manageable for my family that we can maintain saves me mental energy on a daily basis.

Our Family Weekly Rhythm

Sunday	Monday	Tuesday	Wednesday	Thursday	Friday	Saturday
Slow Morning	7:00- M makes breakfast	7:00- M makes breakfast	7:00 - M makes breakfast	7:00- M makes breakfast	7:00- M makes breakfast	8:00- M makes breakfast
8:00- M makes breakfast	Morning Chores Ready for School	Mom Walks Dogs	Homework Morning Chores Ready for School	Mom Walks Dogs	Homework Morning Chores Ready for School	Walk Dogs Chores Mom to Gym
9:15- Get ready for ⛪	8:15 - D takes L+ F to 🏫	7:00- M makes breakfast	8:15- D takes L+ F to 🏫	7:00- M makes breakfast	8:15- D takes L+ F to 🏫	9:00 AM-1:00 PM
9:45- Leave for ⛪	Mom Walks Dogs Dad to Gym	Homework Morning Chores Ready for School	Mom Walks Dogs Dad to Gym	Homework Morning Chores Ready for School	Mom Walks Dogs Dad to Gym	Soccer Games Birthday Party Family Walk
Church Lunch	9:00- M takes B to 🏫	8:15- M takes L+ F to 🏫	9:00- M takes B to 🏫	8:15- M takes L+ F to 🏫	9:00- M takes B to 🏫	1:00-3:00 PM
Down Time Family Time	Mom to Gym	Mom to Gym	9:00-3:00 PM	Mom at Gym	9:00-4:00 PM	Down Time
Playdate Swim in Pool Hobbies	10:00 AM-4:00 PM	9:00- Dad takes B to 🏫	2:00- Dad gets F + L	9:00- D takes B to 🏫	Mom + Dad Work Appointments Mom Runs Errands	3:00 PM-6:00 PM House Projects Family Fun Playdate Errands
	Mom + Dad Work	9:00-4:00 PM	3:00- Mom gets B	9:00-4:00 PM	3:00- Dad gets F + L	
5:00- Family Movie Night	3:00- Dad gets F + L	Mom + Dad Work	Mom at Gym Appointments Snacks + Rest Play w/ Neighbors Dad Works	Mom + Dad Work	4:00- Mom gets B	6:00-9:00 PM
8:00- Get Ready for 🛏	4:00- Mom gets B	3:00- Dad gets F + L		3:00- Dad gets F + L	Snacks + Rest Play w/ Neighbors Mom to Gym Dad Works	Date Night Movie Night Game Night Friends Over
	Snacks + Rest Play w/ Neighbors Mom Chores Dad Works	4:00- Mom gets B	5:00- Early Dinner	4:00- Mom gets B	6:00- Pizza Dinner	9:00, Get Ready for 🛏
	5:00- Early Dinner	Snacks + Rest Play w/ Neighbors Mom Chores Dad Works	5:30- M takes L to Cheer	Snacks + Rest Play w/ Neighbors Mom Chores Dad Works	Low Key Family Movie Night	
	5:30- M + L to cheer, D + F to therapy	5:00- Early Dinner	Dad + Boys Walk Dogs	5:00- Early Dinner	8:00- Get Ready for 🛏	
	8:00- Get Ready for 🛏	5:30- M takes kids to ⚽ + playground	8:00- Get Ready for 🛏	6:00- D takes B to ⚽		
		8:00- Get Ready for 🛏		M + F + L Walk Dogs		
				8:00- Get Ready for 🛏		

For many years I made the mistake of thinking that I could create a weekly routine for my family and then program it in as if I'm a robot that could automatically learn to comply with each intentional piece of my plan. Instead, I've realized that I need to create a weekly flow that accounted for the needs of my family. Basically, I've learned that if something isn't working, it's a lot easier to change the expectation than it is to expect myself to magically start complying. If my weekly flow isn't working, it's usually because my expectations are unrealistic in this season of life and not because I'm failing.

If my weekly flow isn't working, it's usually because my expectations are unrealistic in this season of life and not because I'm a failure.

The weekly flow is only helpful if it's realistic. Some aspects may be a little bit aspirational but for the most part, on a normal week, it should be achievable. Sure, some days there is an urgent work need that I need to address right after drop off instead of going to the gym. That means some days I will skip the gym and other days I might opt to go later in the day. The goal of this weekly flow isn't to create an unrealistic plan you *must* follow, but to be a tool that makes it easier for you to make decisions.

As you create your weekly flow and start implementing it in your life, I encourage you to initially use this tool to learn about your family's natural rhythms. We have different needs for alone time, sleep, spontaneous fun, time with friends, and creative projects. Pay attention to those natural needs as they come up for you and your kids and start planning for them.

Having a weekly flow was especially helpful when my kids were young and weren't in school every day. I needed a plan for what we would do that was realistic for me and flexible but also provided enough engaging activities for my kids. It was never realistic for every day to look the same for me, so it really helped me to have a weekly flow where I could have different activities that I did on different days but on a weekly basis. From week to week my life looked similar, but each specific day had variety.

Over time, as I've done this exercise, it provides a clear visual of how our weeks will generally flow so I know what capacity I have to say yes to new commitments. I've also used this as a tool to learn some things about me and my family that have guided how we live. For example:

- I really like having 1–5 p.m. on Sundays to just be at home and read. Occasionally I'll go to the gym or to HomeGoods, but usually I want to just rest and have downtime. If I don't get that downtime, I'm not as energized on Monday so I try and protect that time.
- My kids and I both need some downtime after school pickups, before going to activities. We can occasionally rally for an appointment but this is the exception and not the norm.
- My kids need physical activity on the weekends if they don't have a sports game or playdate. We try and get them out for a two-mile walk first thing on Saturday and Sunday mornings because it makes the whole day go smoother.
- It's hard for me and my husband to both have productive Saturdays. We must take turns and make plans so that one person is on parent duty, and one is working on projects.
- My kids do best with activities two days a week after school so that they have some afternoons without plans. We prefer earlier activities and like to be home by 6:30 or 7 p.m. if possible. We also prefer activities that are closer to our home, which has informed what activities we pursue.
- I myself don't like to be out of the house more than one night a week for personal commitments. I have one weekly event on Mondays during the school year but rarely make plans beyond that.
- My whole family is hungry for dinner early so if we can't be home by 6 p.m., we prefer to have dinner at 4:30 or 5 p.m. Waiting until 7 p.m. for dinner always backfires with very hangry kids. On those nights, I keep meals super simple.
- My mental energy isn't great in the evenings and my kids get up early. For my younger kids, homework usually gets done in the mornings after they take their medicine.

The goal of thinking through your weekly flow is for you to ease the chaos of your home even more and for you to create a predictable routine that works for your family. Routine is one of those things that is so helpful for those of us with ADHD and our kids, but it can be hard to create and to maintain. I think it's much easier to aim for predictability for you and for your family. It's really the same thing as routine but for some reason it doesn't give me the same allergic reaction.

This exercise also improved my communication with my spouse and enabled me to delegate more. It's easier for both of us to have consistent expectations. If he's taking our oldest to soccer every Tuesday and Thursday, I don't need to remind him about that or worry about that happening. If he has a conflict, we navigate that but we aren't deciding each week who is taking Bowman to soccer. This is the automated part!

Predictability means your kids know when they will have time to do their homework. It means they know when they will get to be on screens. It means they know when they need to leave for certain activities. It means they know when they will get unstructured time to spend time with friends or pursue a hobby or interest. Predictability goes a long way for you (and your spouse!) in managing the many details of your home and family, but it's a hugely helpful tool for your neurodivergent kids as well.

> *Predictability goes a long way for you (and your spouse!) in managing the many details of your home and family, but it's a hugely helpful tool for your neurodivergent kids as well.*

The goal in creating a weekly flow for you and your family is to let go of what you think your routine or lifestyle "should" look like and start prioritizing the actual needs of the people in your home. I know this is easier said than done and accepting the unique needs of your neurodivergent family can be an ongoing long-term thing that continues to pop up even after you think you've got it figured out.

But let go of expecting your family to conform to the "right" weekly schedule and instead start getting curious about what you and your family need to thrive. Use the weekly flow as a tool to lighten your mental load and make decisions about your life, and pay attention to what is working and what isn't. Only you and your family can decide the right weekly flow for your unique family.

Lean into Technology

Once you get a feel for your normal weekly flow, you can take what you've learned about your family and the decisions that you've made in the previous steps and start leaning into technology.

Personally, I'm not a fan of separate checklist apps for your phone, though if you've found tools that work for you, don't let me stop you. For me, pulling up my phone is a recipe for disaster. I get easily sidetracked by either swiping through Instagram or adding things to my Amazon cart.

Instead, what's worked for me is keeping it simple. I use printed and laminated checklists to track my progress and use technology to provide an additional layer of accountability and support.

For checklists, I still prefer my laminated paper versions rather than anything on my phone. I get an extra dopamine boost by checking it off and I really like the visual of seeing the list getting completed each week and month.

That said, I do rely heavily on my online calendar and alarms on my phone and watch.

Each season, when I update my weekly flow, I go through and update my electronic calendar with all the relevant times and create recurring events. I use Apple calendar, and those events sync to my phone, my watch, my electronic calendar, and my computer. When I look at my calendar, I see the plans for the week and not a blank schedule. If I need to make small adjustments each week, I do that, but I usually don't change much.

I add two reminders for each event, one for an hour before and one for when we need to leave. I always add the addresses for recurring activities so that my watch can tell me how long it will take to get there. For events where I need to leave at specific time, I set up specific recurring alarms on my phone to prompt me to leave, and I often add notes.

Alarm Examples from My Real Life

- Start getting ready
- Start working
- Stop working—10 mins to leave for pickups
- Walk the dogs
- Leave for the gym
- Leave to walk L and F to school
- Leave to take B to school
- Leave to pick up B from school

- Make an afternoon smoothie or snack for the kids
- Start making dinner
- Leave to take F to tennis
- Leave to take B to soccer
- Leave to take L to cheer
- Start bedtime routine for kids
- Start getting ready for church
- Leave for church

I have learned to embrace redundancy. I need *all* the reminders that I can get because my brain easily forgets my commitments, weekly tasks, and monthly tasks. I teach this system every day of my life and still must look at my monthly task list to see what I decided was important to me last time I updated it. I don't trust myself to remember what time I need to get ready for church or what time I need to leave to get my son from school and instead I've learned to plan for those struggles by leaning into technology.

If you are expecting your days to be filled to the brim with taxing tasks that your brain hates, you won't be able to maintain it and your brain will continue to rebel against any sort of structure.

If you are expecting your days to be filled to the brim with taxing tasks that your brain hates, you won't be able to maintain it and your brain will continue to rebel against any sort of structure. You will find nonurgent side projects to pursue. You will get stuck in paralysis. You will feel like a failure because you've set yourself up with unrealistic expectations.

Your daily rhythm and your weekly flow should all be reflected in your electronic calendar. If you are getting the stimulation, exercise, challenge, rest, and fun that you need and your children are getting the predictability that they need, your ideal lifestyle will start to take shape. It will get easier to determine what gets your time and energy and to have clarity as you make decisions on an ongoing basis. You will have more mental clarity, and your creativity and self-confidence will skyrocket.

Step 7 Application: Using whatever tool is easiest for you, map out your weekly flow for your current season of life. You can using the template provided at https://www.amymariehann.com/mtmbook or use my Canva templates available for purchase at www.amymariehann.com for more customization options. This shouldn't include every detail of your life but is more a rough overview of how your weeks will look. Think of this as a tool that you could give to a spouse or family member who needs to know your availability. You should plan to tweak your weekly flow at the start of each new season (August, January and May) as seasonal commitments, activities and school schedules change. You can print this out as a reference tool, but the real value in creating the weekly flow is in the actual exercise of creating it.

Once you have your weekly flow, your daily rhythm, and your weekly and monthly tasks, make sure that they are reflected on your electronic calendar. Set up recurring alarms on your phone for all relevant times when you know will need an additional prompt or reminder to follow through on tasks.

# 12 | Troubleshooting

Let me make things a lot easier as you attempt to manage life with ADHD. It's probably going to piss you off a little bit because it's dang annoying, but the sooner you accept this *one* simple truth, the happier that you will be in every area of your life.

Are you ready for it? Okay, here it is.

I apologize in advance because I really do hate being the one to break this to you.

> *Every ADHD strategy that works for you will eventually get boring and not work anymore.*

Every ADHD strategy that works for you will eventually get boring and not work anymore.

Sigh. I know, right? Big old bummer.

Some take this to mean that they are simply incapable of change and should just stop trying because it's futile, but that's not you because you've already made it nearly to the end of this book. So let me elaborate on what does work.

You must stop beating yourself up when one strategy no longer works for you and instead develop a full arsenal of options that you can easily deploy. And if, like me, you are the ringleader of multiple neurodivergent offspring, the more tools you have in your arsenal, the better able you'll be able to support them. Because Lord knows their ADHD will present in very different ways to keep you on your toes.

So let me introduce to you the 10 strategies or concepts that have helped me the most in learning to manage my ADHD when I need to switch things up.

Seasonal Planning

As I live out the MTM system for myself and my family, I rely heavily on what I call "seasonal planning." It's really a chance to update and tweak all my lists so that they are more relevant and to create a little novelty.

A great thing about ADHD brains is that we love to find better ways to do things and are constantly creating new solutions. But this can easily lead us to waste lots of energy tweaking and changing things, and can prevent us from every getting to the implementing. Seasonal planning helps me get around this. Occasionally I'll tweak my lists and print out and laminate a new version, but I've found it's more helpful to do that with every new season.

As a mom, my life changes the most at the start of the school year, after the holidays, and then at the start of summer. I set aside time with each of these new seasons to update my life.

This might look like:

- Updating my weekly and monthly task lists if anything has changed. I might just move around the days of when I do things to create some variety.
- Updating my monthly calendar with all the dates that I know about with the goal of keeping one extra per day.
- Updating my weekly flow to reflect any schedule changes or new goals.
- Updating my electronic calendar to reflect the changes to my weekly flow.
- Updating my alarms to reflect the schedule changes.
- Update and print my Mom Admin list for the upcoming season.
- Update my meal plan rotation to avoid boredom.

Yes, this takes time and intentionality, but it lowers my daily stress immensely. It's a thousand times easier to make decisions for the next three to four months during one block of time so that I have fewer decisions to make daily. I even host a community "seasonal planning session" my membership community for each new season as a source of accountability for myself and all the members.

Simplifying

Um, duh. This one doesn't need a ton of explanation, or does it?

When I was deep in my burnout season trying to spin all the plates and do it all perfectly, this was the hardest one for me to really embrace. And yet simplifying is the most important initial strategy to employ.

At the core, simplifying is really learning what matters to you and your family and letting go of everything that doesn't. A few years ago, I stumbled on a few Instagram accounts all about minimalism and I was fascinated and intrigued. I loved the aesthetic and immediately wanted specifics on how to achieve minimalist status. I wanted numbers, rules, and a checklist to follow to simplify my life. Really, I wanted to know how to get an A+ in simplification and minimalism because surely there were grades and rules, and I wanted to know them.

But over time, I've come to adopt a much less structured viewpoint on minimalism. I don't think it's about how many bowls or spoons you have; it's really about giving yourself permission to focus on a few areas of your life and to put other areas on the back burner for the time being. I can make significant progress in my life, but I have to be intentional about how many areas I'm trying to address at one time.

For me, it means opting out of things that aren't a priority in this season of life. It's letting go of what other people think and listening to my own intuition. It's picking my battles with my kids and letting the minor things go.

It's also about looking to make things *simple* and avoiding my tendency to overcomplicate things. I'm great at making things complicated and fancy. It's part of having a creative brain that loves big ideas. Simplifying has meant dreaming big but then learning to execute small-scale versions that are more manageable.

Simplifying has required me to address many fears and insecurities. Not everyone understands the choices that we make and how we live our lives. At the same time, simplifying has meant that I feel more myself than ever before and the friends that I have made in the process are that much deeper.

For me this looks like:

- Letting go of attempts to create the perfect ADHD-friendly home-school environment and choosing to send the kids to public school.

- Taking on fewer professional projects so that I can see them to completion.
- Caring a lot less about brand names and fashion trends for me and my kids.
- Opting out of volunteer work for seasons.
- Taking breaks from kid's activities for seasons.
- Taking a break from family travel for seasons.
- Choosing small family birthday celebrations instead of elaborate birthday parties.
- Pursuing fewer projects around the house and hiring a handyman to complete the few things we decide are priorities.
- Shopping at fewer stores and opting for grocery delivery whenever possible.

Breaking It Down

I've shared extensively about my need for challenge and how I've realized that having one big challenge is much more rewarding and manageable for me than having many smaller challenges. For many years, getting overwhelmed by the many steps of larger challenges made it hard for me to pursue my big goals. Though I had big ideas, it was hard for me to take action when I felt like my time was so limited.

I've gotten much better at breaking all my goals down into actionable steps. I now realize that it is worth my while to slow down and think through the steps before acting so that I break things down into smaller steps. This has enabled me to make tremendous progress toward my goals without having to have huge chunks of uninterrupted time.

I now apply this strategy to pretty much everything I do in life. I know that I must break every goal into smaller specific tasks that I can check off as I go. For the ongoing weekly work of running my business, I have my weekly goals broken into specific subtasks that I accomplish each week. It keeps me feeling motivated and with a clear plan for what I'm doing to reach my big goals.

ADHD brains don't produce the same sense of job satisfaction that neurotypical brains do. Our brains forget what we've accomplished, and it can be an ongoing challenge to feel like we are making progress toward our goals. We must create ways to recognize the steps that we are taking and to celebrate our progress.

Delayed gratification is also hard for us! So breaking things down and celebrating the progress along the way is how we keep the motivation to keep moving when we get bored or it gets hard.

Breaking It Down

PROJECT

☐

SUBTASKS:

☐ ☐ ☐ ☐

Breaking down our goals is its own way of simplifying. When tasks are too complicated and overwhelming, we are prone to tune them out and avoid them. Dividing large projects or goals into smaller subtasks enables us to focus just on that one specific subtask, as opposed to getting paralyzed by the larger project.

Additionally, our energy and focus may not last as long as our neurotypical counterparts. I have found that it's much more effective to break big projects down and then to focus on progress over sticking to any specific pace. As I write this book, it's easier for me to focus on writing for two to four hours and let that be my goal than it is to track some specific word count every time I sit down. Each small act of progress helps.

Whether my goals are professional or personal, it helps me to focus on breaking it down into the smaller subtasks that I want to do and then focus on working my way through the list of subtasks. The subtasks need to be specific and interesting enough that completing them will feel rewarding.

For example, writing for 15–30 minutes is not rewarding, but getting out of my house for a two- or three-hour writing session is much more satisfying. Initially, when I planned out how I would divide up this book, I set goals for completing specific chapters on specific days. In practice, that didn't work, and I needed to shift to tracking my writing sessions and trust that if I kept making progress, I would get to my goal. In every new endeavor I pursue, I must find the right size of subtasks.

Sometimes the subtasks are in measures of time but often it's specific tasks. As I plan my expectations for my work on an ongoing basis, this practice has been life-changing. I tend to have incredibly big goals and unrealistic ideas of how much I can accomplish on a given day or in each week. Getting clear on what subtasks I can accomplish each week has allowed me to make substantial progress and has made it easier to understand what goals or projects are for now and what are for the future when I have more time or capacity. Here's a general overview of how this works for me. I try and tackle two of these tasks a day and then have wiggle room for some random idea or need that pops up.

Breaking It Down

PROJECT

Weekly Business Tasks

SUBTASKS:

Update Finances & Tracking	Plan All Social Media Posts	Host Weekly Coaching Call	Send Weekly Newsletter	Deep Work Writing Session
	Record Video Content	Edit All Video Content	Collaboration or Podcast Interview	Technology & Funnel Tweaks

It helps me to have these subtasks thought out for the foreseeable future because I spend very little time planning my work time each week. I know what needs to get done and have spread the tasks out throughout my week so I'm making progress but also have variety so that I don't get bored. I also give myself small rewards for the subtasks that are harder or more draining. For example, I'm always tired after hosting a group coaching call, so I usually watch a show while I eat my lunch.

As you consider the challenges you want to pursue, consider how you can break that challenge down into the size of subtask that works with your life. For example, if you are pursuing this goal during your daughter's two-hour daily nap, make sure each subtask can be completed within two hours. It is probably unrealistic to assume that you'd be able to complete seven of these two-hour subtasks in any given week, but two or three subtasks per week may be a more appropriate goal. As you learn to pursue these challenging subtasks, you will get much more efficient and able to get farther toward your goals than you anticipate.

Break your goals and challenges into the right-size subtasks so you feel energized and accomplished as each subtask is completed. I highly recommend having an actual visual that you can check off. Hello, dopamine boost! You want to feel forward momentum without getting stuck in paralysis or overwhelmed by how far you have left to go.

Chunking

Chunking is one of my favorite strategies for managing things in my home. At this point, I've pretty much hammered home the idea that ADHD brains prefer hard to easy, and chunking is where we take that idea and run with it. We embrace that harder is easier for us and we'd rather chunk small, easy tasks together to make them harder. We then get one larger task that is going to feel more rewarding once completed and give us a bigger dopamine boost.

So many of the tips and strategies around home management are designed to make things easier for us by breaking things into small tasks. This is one reason why those of us with ADHD can feel so much shame and embarrassment because these small, easy tasks are so hard for us.

> *Wash your bowl and spoon right after you use them.*
> *Wash one load of laundry, fold it, and put it away each day.*
> *Find an easy 30-minute dinner idea that you can make tonight.*

But for my brain, small tasks are so much harder because they provide so little dopamine, and they require a lot of motivation to get me started. It's not an efficient use of my energy, which is why chunking has been a better alternative.

As I created the MTM system, chunking was an important part of it. I realized that I needed to find the right-sized chunks for the tasks in my life so that I could stay on top of them in a way that worked for me. Trying to do everything daily was just not realistic, but chunking things into weekly and monthly tasks was a lot easier for my brain. Larger, harder chunks were actually easier for me to complete which made it easier for me to be consistent.

I started chunking with laundry. For me, washing clothes is not that hard, but it's the folding and putting them away that's so painful. Folding each load felt excruciating, but folding a massive basket of laundry once a week seemed much easier and more rewarding. It takes me about 45 minutes to fold a week's worth of laundry, so I can put on a show that I love and make it more of a fun thing than a daily task that I dread.

The downside to this method is that our clothes do get a little more wrinkled. For a while I let that go and embraced what worked for me even if it wasn't perfect. In time I started ironing our nicer items once a month while watching a show or movie. Ironing isn't my favorite but I've been able to stay on top of it as a monthly task.

I also started chunking meal planning and meal prep. Planning meals out every week was super stressful for me. I found planning meals for the month or even for two weeks at a time to be a lot easier. I have a monthly meal plan that doesn't change much each month.

I make a few minor tweaks as we get sick of things, but I have a rotation of meals over the month that I can cook through. If those meals are feeling boring, I'll change it up during my seasonal planning session. Doing this weekly is too much for me, but a few times a year I can handle. Once a month, I'll do a big shop and then prep a bunch of meals for the freezer.

This process takes a lot of time and energy, but the feeling when my freezer is fully stocked and I don't have to think about what to make for the rest of the month is truly amazing. It's a huge dopamine rush and feels so incredibly good to have gotten it accomplished. Though some may think this sounds way too hard, for me harder is easier and this method just works.

The key to chunking is giving yourself permission to embrace the "harder is easier" mindset and playing with your tasks to find what works for you and your family. There's no right way of doing life and your ADHD brain will probably find a unique way to chunk things that never occurred to me.

Front-Loading

Nope, I'm not talking about a washing machine. And in case you care, I'm a top-loader girlie. The stinky smell of the front-loaders isn't for me. Gross.

Front-loading is the most helpful to me when it comes to managing money but also impacts how I manage my energy too. Front-loading is just intentionally spending on priority concerns or needs you know about right away so that you've taken care of the necessary things first.

Basically, I pay myself every two weeks and I try to order and purchase anything I know we will need for those two weeks right away. This strategy was also why I started doing the bulk meal prep because it was easier for me to budget if I got the grocery shopping out of the way, so I'd know how much I had to work with for the rest of the period. I then order gifts or things that I know we'll need for the next two weeks. If there are some things in my cart I've been wanting to order, I base those decisions on how much is left.

This strategy has helped me to avoid overspending and impulse spending, but it's also helped me to think ahead in many ways. I'm not scrambling on a Saturday morning to go get a present for a kid's birthday party or running to the sports store to buy a new soccer ball for practice. It helps me to prioritize needs and to avoid that daily stress.

As I think about planning my time, I take this same approach. I prioritize my business subtasks that need to happen before I pursue some random idea. I use what time is left to pursue those other things. I also try to plan out months, first blocking out the necessary tasks (like doctor's appointments, going to Costco, and haircuts), before making plans for fun outings or playdates.

My brain really struggles with knowing how much money I have and knowing how much time and energy I have. Front-loading is a simple strategy that has helped me to stay ahead of myself to avoid getting depleted and overspending.

Outsourcing

I have mixed feelings about outsourcing. On one hand, I'm a huge fan and believe that you should have zero guilt for outsourcing as your finances allow, but on the other hand, raising neurodivergent kids is expensive. Medicine, doctor appointments, evaluations, therapists, supplements . . . it all adds up, and I understand that outsourcing, in the traditional use of the word, is just not financially feasible for many families.

In the traditional sense, outsourcing is paying someone else to complete tasks that you don't have the skills, time, or energy to complete. These days you can outsource so many things: cleaning, meal preparation, yard work, laundering clothes, event planning, childcare, carpet cleaning, house projects, home repairs, organizing, pet care, car cleaning. In an ideal world you'd be able to pay someone else to do all the taxing tasks that you tend to avoid.

When I hit my wall and was deep in ADHD burnout, we didn't have the finances to outsource much. There was room to outsource one thing, and my main priority was childcare. I knew that I needed a break from my children and so we sent my youngest to preschool while the older boys were in school. That allowed me to grow my business, which has enabled me in time to outsource more.

I created the MTM system because I had to figure out a way to manage most of the taxing tasks between me and my husband while also parenting our neurodivergent kids well. If you are there, know that you aren't alone, and that outsourcing is just *one* of the strategies discussed in this chapter for a reason.

For many the barrier to outsourcing is in the executive functioning required to set up a service provider. If you can afford a cleaner, the challenge can be finding one and then setting it up. That requires executive functioning.

As you create your weekly and monthly tasks, identify areas of your life that you'd like to outsource and aim to set up one new provider a month. You might also go to a coffee shop with your spouse and work on this together, finding providers, texting friends for recommendations, making phone calls, and then determining which of you is the point person.

If you find someone available and taking new clients, schedule the appointment. If you have someone on the phone, use that momentum while you have it. They might not be the perfect provider, but you can always schedule someone else down the road if you find a better fit. I encourage you to set up each new provider to come at the same time and day of the week so that it's more predictable for you.

When you're considering what to outsource and what you can afford, I encourage you to lean into your values. We've recently hired someone to clean our home once a week after many years of me doing it by myself. Though we now have more financial breathing room, it's still a choice that we are intentionally making. We have a family of homebodies who enjoy being in our home and I for one love for it to be clean. It takes so much stress and anxiety off my plate and puts me in a better mood. I'm a better mom when someone else is cleaning my house regularly.

I'd rather cut back on eating out in order to have a cleaning lady. I'd rather cut back on buying new clothes to have a cleaning lady. I'd rather skip getting my nails done to have a cleaning lady. I'd rather make my own coffee to have a cleaning lady. I'd even rather skip elaborate family vacations to have a cleaning lady.

I value my home being a peaceful and calm place for me and my family, so the investment in a weekly cleaning lady is in line with my values and priorities. There is a lot that I'm willing to let go to make that a regular priority. You will likely need to cut back in some areas of your life to invest in outsourcing. Focus first on those areas that most align with your values and priorities because they will bring you the most benefit.

If outsourcing ongoing tasks like cleaning isn't financially feasible, try outsourcing smaller projects or needs on a quarterly or semi-annual basis. One of the first things I began to outsource was hiring a handyman a few times a year to complete a list of projects that I wanted to tackle. For many years I had an expectation that my husband should be able to devote his weekends to my project requests, but as our kids have gotten older, we both spend most of the weekend in parent mode. He is an incredibly present and involved partner in raising our kids, and I realize now that I can't expect him to be both the dad on duty and paint the guest room. Hiring someone to knock out my wish list helps both of us.

As I look to the future and set goals for myself and my business, many of them are around outsourcing. My personal desire is to use my gifts and resources to help others and care well for my family. As my income grows, I don't plan to get a bigger house, fancier car, or more stuff, because that will only lead to *more* executive functioning and maintenance. I aim to create more capacity for myself and my husband in time as I'm able to outsource as much as possible so that I can use my mental and physical energy in more meaningful ways.

Body Doubling

The power of body doubling continues to surprise me. It is the easiest strategy to employ and the most consistently helpful.

Body doubling is a productivity strategy where you work alongside another person to help you stay on task and focus on your goal. It can be done in person, over the phone, or on a computer. The other person might be speaking to you, or you may have headphones on and not actually talking to each other. How it looks really depends on the context and the task.

Body doubling can look as simple as talking to a girlfriend while you are doing the dishes. Some women in my membership community have a specific friend they Facetime on a consistent basis to keep each other accountable with daily boring tasks. You might have an actual conversation, or you might simply keep each other company.

It can also look like sitting on your son's bed while he puts his laundry away. Even if he's still doing the task by himself, your physical presence will be helpful to him in initiating the task. You may also sit and read a book while a child does their homework. You don't have to be actively participating to be helpful. It's important that you have calm energy and aren't adding stress.

I use body doubling most frequently around managing and tracking money. For many years I'd try to block out my time by assigning a specific time of the week to update our budget tracking and money situation. And then every week that time would come and go without me sitting down to update said budget. The more I procrastinated and avoided this task, the more shame I felt, which did nothing to help my insecurity around money.

Body doubling has been life-changing in two ways for me when it comes to managing money. Initially, my husband and I started having weekly money check-ins with the sole goal of starting to talk about money. We then started using this time to update our budget and track our spending.

It turns out that all along I really needed this extra level of support to make myself do this task. Accepting that about myself and allowing for this accommodation has been incredibly helpful. Left to my own devices, I will never get around to updating the budget and I need him to keep me accountable.

My husband also benefits from this time because he has similar struggles. We lean on each other and know that we both need the accountability to do this essential task for our family. For years we tried to push it back to the other person to manage, but we both need the expectation to sit down to look at our finances.

Additionally, I currently host a two-hour time blocking session for my membership community. Whoever wants to participate logs in from their computers or phones, and we each do tasks that we tend to avoid. This is when I do my financial tracking for my business and look at my numbers and progress. I also clean out my inbox from the weekend and plan out social media posts for the week.

These three tasks are incredibly helpful to the life of my business and help my weeks run much smoother. For some reason, starting work on Monday is always especially hard for me even though I love what I do. Having this built-in appointment to log in on Mondays at noon has helped me to make these habits consistent, which has led to significant success in my business.

Among the women I work with, I've noticed a huge desire to serve, encourage, and help others. So many women with ADHD are more willing to show up for others than they are willing to show up for themselves. We often struggle with following through with our own goals but are more likely to follow through when someone else is impacted. This is where body doubling can be helpful on an ongoing basis.

Learning to thrive with ADHD starts with owning our own tendencies and then finding ways to accommodate those instead of wishing for them to magically change. Self-awareness is much more effective than self-control. As you identify ongoing tendencies that you struggle to address, consider how body doubling might help you finally create change.

Developing Autonomy

You probably don't know me in real life. (If you do, thanks for reading!) But if we haven't met, there's one thing you should know: I'm not really an athlete.

Sure, I love to exercise and work out regularly, but I'm not exactly what you'd call coordinated. And I don't have a "runner's body," whatever that's supposed to mean. My flat feet can trigger a plantar fasciitis flare-up if I even think about running too much (kidding, not kidding).

But in my late 20s, I ran the Marine Corps Marathon in Washington, DC.

Why? Good question. It was just something I had always wanted to do, and I happened to be in a season of life when I had the time and energy to devote to training. I had recently moved to a new city, didn't have much going on, and thought, why not?

I started training but I did it my way.

- I found a coaching protocol that fit me perfectly—a run/walk combo that felt doable for a novice like me.
- I did every single training run by myself because running with others gave me anxiety. (Keeping up with other people's paces? No thank you!) Running solo gave me the freedom to go at my own pace—slow as molasses.
- I picked my own charity and even had my race day shirt custom-made.

On race day, my now-husband was there to cheer me on, and a few friends joined in, but mostly I ran my race, at my pace, doing my run/walk combo just as I had trained.

And here's the thing: I was so slow. I don't even remember my time, but I do remember that by the time I crossed the finish line, they were literally tearing it all down.

But I freaking did it. I crossed that finish line. And no one can ever take that accomplishment away from me.

Looking back, that marathon was more than just a physical challenge. It was a perfect example of how I approach the things that really matter in life:

- I always need to find my own way.
- I need the freedom to go at my own pace—whether I'm moving faster or slower than others.
- I must do what works for me.
- I need to be self-motivated.

Once I'm motivated, though? Watch out. I'm deeply determined.

I didn't realize it at the time, but this was my autonomy in action. I had a goal I cared about, I figured out the process that worked for me, and I stuck with it—even if it didn't look the way other people thought it "should."

It took me much longer to realize that the same principles would apply to my journey as a mom with ADHD. Parenting and adulting come with their own challenges, and I've learned—sometimes the hard way—that autonomy is nonnegotiable.

That's why it's so important to figure out what works for you. It's also why it might feel like you can't consistently implement any one strategy or system. If it doesn't make sense to your ADHD brain, align with your values, or account for the unique needs of your family, it isn't going to work for you long term. You might get intrigued for a few weeks, but it won't really stick.

> *For those of us with ADHD, autonomy isn't just a preference; it's a survival tool. We thrive when we have the freedom to follow our interests, structure our lives in ways that make sense to us, and pursue our goals on our own terms.*

Stop beating yourself up for not being able to manage your home, your time, and your energy like you think you "should," and instead get obsessed with finding what works for you and your brain. Give yourself full autonomy to find your own unique way. Everything I share in this book is designed to get your juices flowing with the understanding that we are different people with different families and different circumstances. The system that you land on will look different from mine because we are different people.

So many women want me to provide an easy-to-follow cleaning list or task list of the "right way" to do things and to live well as a mom with ADHD. It doesn't work that way. This process takes more time, but it also leads to transformational change.

> *Give yourself full autonomy to find your own unique way.*

Transformation isn't a quick business, and it isn't based on doing things the "right way" to check off all the boxes. It must be motivated by your values and deep desires for your life and family.

Delegating

One of the most common questions I get initially is around what it looks like to include your spouse and children in implementing the system. My answer always surprises people. Delegation is essential but I think it's hard to implement before you've done the necessary work of really understanding your capacity.

By delegation, I mean assigning tasks to your children through chores and assigning specific tasks to your spouse to manage. These are both important, but they are much more complicated in neurodivergent families.

In terms of chores, expecting my neurodivergent children to complete tasks in a timely manner without my oversight or direction is futile. At the time of this writing, my children are 14, 10, and 6. My oldest does many things to help me daily, like making his lunch, taking out the trash, making a meal for his siblings, and making his bed. He can do those chores without oversight and usually complies right away. He does, however, still need to be prompted to do them. My younger children need a lot more management and instruction.

In raising neurodivergent kids, it's imperative that you realize that your expectations around what they "should" be able to do at various ages may be very different from what they are able to do at that age. In his book *12 Principles for Raising a Child with ADHD,* Dr. William Barclay explains that children with ADHD are often delayed by 30%. This means that my 10-year-old son has the maturity of a seven-year-old in many areas of his life. When considering what chores or tasks your children can take on, it's important to look at their actual abilities and to let go of your preconceived notions. Focus on growing their skills where they are, as opposed to expecting them to be able to meet a specific demand because of their age.

As a parent, I will admit that this is incredibly frustrating. I wish that I could create an elaborate chore chart where I assign the tasks of managing our home to every member of our family and then those tasks get magically completed without my oversight or management. I spent many, many years trying to invent this exact system, only to realize that this never actually worked for me and my family. We could never follow through with it and I was left feeling like a failure for not being able to enforce the system for my kids.

It was pointless for me to think that I could expect my ADHD kids to independently make themselves complete the boring tasks that I was incapable of making myself complete. Instead, I needed to first learn to make myself do the boring things and then help my kids implement those same strategies for doing their chores.

For my family, that has mostly looked like having minimal, very clear responsibilities for my children. I ask that they make their bed, hang up their towels, and put their laundry in the hamper. I don't expect perfect adherence, and I accept that they may need many reminders. I have visual reminders throughout our home to remind them of these expectations and provide checklists for any detailed request, like cleaning any room of the house.

> *It was pointless for me to think that I could expect my ADHD kids to independently make themselves complete the boring tasks that I was incapable of making myself complete.*

It takes a lot of time and intentional parenting before my children become helpful in managing the home tasks. If they require oversight or management in any way, I don't really think of it as delegation because it's still on my mental radar. And I don't expect assigning chores to my kids or creating a list of things they "should" be able to do an effective solution to lightening my mental load. Been there, done that, and it just didn't work.

In terms of involving my kids in completing my tasks, I found that it's helpful to focus on incorporating them in my tasks. If I were to assign them a list of three or four weekly tasks beyond my weekly tasks and then I was trying to manage those, that would push me over my daily six to seven taxing tasks. Instead, I think about incorporating them into my tasks. For example, they go to the car wash with me and help clean out the car and wipe down their seats. They might also help me with any of my cleaning tasks, and I'll call them in to be a helper whenever possible.

So, in general, I include my kids to make them kind, helpful humans but don't look to them to make my daily life easier. Accepting that hard truth was pretty life-changing for how I parent and helped me to appreciate them more for helping and to celebrate the growth as it comes.

With my husband, delegation has been life-changing for our marriage. Mark is also ADHD and has many of the same struggles around boring things that I do. Like me, he also really benefits from autonomy and needs to find his own way of doing things.

When I created this system, it really helped me to focus just on myself initially. This always surprises people, but I think it was one of the things that helped me the most in creating lasting change. I focused first on understanding my capacity and my needs so that I could then create clear boundaries and expectations for myself.

In our marriage, I am the doer and the one with unrealistic expectations. My tendency has always been to expect more than humanely possible of both me and my husband. For me, starting with delegation would have been a recipe for disaster because I would have imposed a long list of unrealistic tasks on my husband, which would have left us both discouraged and defeated.

Instead, in time, as I've come to let go of my unrealistic expectations, I am now an expert at what I can handle and what I need. This has led to me having much more realistic expectations for my spouse, delegating specific areas to him, and giving him full autonomy of his responsibilities.

Old me would have had very high expectations and need to micromanage how he executed those responsibilities, which meant he was pretty much guaranteed to feel like a failure. It also wouldn't have lightened my mental load because I was still worrying about how and when he was doing the tasks that I wanted him to do.

New me has boundaries and knows that if an area of our life is under his domain, I don't have the bandwidth to worry about it. He gets to manage that task how it best suits him, and I give him my support and confidence. If he needs my help or partnership in some way, I'm there but I no longer try to micromanage him.

I share all of this with you because delegation, though so helpful, was not easy for me. I had to do a lot of internal work before I could really get to the place where I could delegate without micromanaging him. And when I stopped micromanaging, it became much easier for him to find his own systems.

For our marriage, we've found that in general it's a lot easier for us each to own different areas of our life on an ongoing basis. We do best with routine and predictability. Where some families share the daily load around dinner, that's more in my domain. If I need Mark to step in and take it over, he can and will, but he's not worrying daily about what groceries we have or what we are cooking for dinner. If we were both thinking about that daily, it would mean more executive functioning for both of us.

In our home, my husband manages the yard, the pool, all home repairs (including scheduling appointments), school communication, all technology issues, pet food, trash, getting bath time started, putting our boys to bed, cleaning his office, sport sign-ups for the boys, drop off and pick-ups on specific days, and paying all bills. There are a few things that we both manage, like parenting and discipline issues, but because he has clear areas of control and full autonomy of how those things get done, it means that I don't worry about his areas at all.

He has full access to my lists and systems and I'm always glad to create a tool for him if he asks me to, but I do not tell him when or what to do. That would mean management and oversight from me. He's my partner and equal and just as he doesn't micromanage how I carry out my tasks, I give him the same level of autonomy. I don't try to assert my systems on him and don't expect myself to manage his ADHD.

One woman mentioned taking the "mom admin" idea and creating a "dad admin" list for her spouse. I'll be honest—I haven't done that. It's not that only a "mom" should be responsibility for these tasks, but instead that I have learned not to impose my expectations on my husband. This feels more like management than delegation to me. And if I'm managing something, that means it's taking up my EFs and limiting my capacity.

I love the idea of him having a "dad admin" list and would gladly help him think through that if asked, but I won't be creating that for him or assigning him specific tasks to complete. He still has seasonal tasks on his radar but he gets to decide how he tracks and manages his responsibilities. I've been married to him for 17 years and know that his demand avoidance would *not* like that and it would actually make him less likely to be involved.

Unfortunately, I understand that for many people, delegating tasks to their spouse feels a lot like creating that wishful chore chart for ADHD kids. It sounds great in theory, but there is no follow-through on their part and you end up still managing everything. I wish I could dig deeper to understand your story and offer more personalized advice, but I encourage you to lean into the other strategies shared here and, more importantly, to pursue personalized support to navigate your marital challenges.

If you are meeting all the needs for your home and family by yourself, that really sucks and I'm sorry. But I encourage you to focus first on getting yourself out of burnout and overwhelm. Your spouse being unsupportive or unwilling to participate doesn't mean life needs to keep going like it's going. You can take steps to simplify, lower your ongoing stress, and better care for yourself.

Sharing the management of our home with my spouse didn't come quickly and easily and involved a lot of humility and personal growth from both of us. My husband was diagnosed with autism and has been in ongoing weekly therapy for the last five years. I want to encourage you that change is possible. That change starts with you understanding your brain, your needs, and your capacity so that you can advocate for yourself.

How you delegate different areas of responsibilities in your home and family may look very different in your home. There is not one right way of how responsibilities should be divvied up, and your dynamic and gifts may be very different from ours. What matters most is that you get really clear on your personal capacity and learning to manage your own ADHD so that you can communicate your needs to your spouse.

Using Music

I rely on music significantly to manage my ADHD, to stay on task, and to motivate myself to do things that I don't want to do. On the most basic level, music helps make my life more fun and stimulates dopamine, but I've found it to be so much more than that. Three kinds of music help me function each day. I think of them as focus music, hype music, and mellow music.

I started listening to focus music a few years ago and I truly can't work without it. I have noise-blocking earbuds and a go-to play list on Apple Music that I listen to called Pure Focus. I searched focus music and found this playlist and haven't looked back.

There are different kinds of focus music, and my husband has a different playlist he prefers that is mostly binaural beats. There is lots of interesting research around the power of music to increase concentration and focus while decreasing distractions. Some prefer classical music, and others prefer low-fi music.

The science around why focus music helps is above my paygrade, but I'd encourage you to try out a few options and find a specific playlist that helps you focus. Pull up this playlist when you need to sit down at your computer or tackle a complicated task. It will help you be more productive, stay focused, and lower your stress.

Hype music is probably already a no-brainer for you. I'm a huge fan of '90s hip hop and have several favorite playlists that I love to sing loud and proud. A few months ago I created a personalized playlist that I call "AMH Memories" of songs that are associated with various happy memories of mine throughout my life.

A Mel Robbins podcast on the science of music gave me this idea, and it's been so helpful. I've been listening to this playlist during workouts and when I need to pump myself up for a complicated creative task. It's basically like a little shot of serotonin that makes me happy and resets my mood. It has also been helpful in remembering and processing different seasons of my life.

The last kind of music that I've been leaning in to more and more is mellow music. I'm typically very much a sensory seeker and I tend to prefer loud, fun, fast songs that get me singing and dancing. My brain needs stimulation and for many years I've been pulling up fun music to get me moving.

As a mom, I find that this gets complicated, and the faster, louder, music, especially in the afternoons and evenings, can get me overstimulated. My husband and oldest son are more sensory avoiders so sometimes my loud, fast music can be really dysregulating to them. When we're in the car in the afternoons or evening as a family, I've found that intentionally listening to mellower music is helpful to everyone. I get the stimulation that I need without getting overstimulated and my son and husband don't get dysregulated.

I'm sure there is some fancy scientific reason to explain how this mellow music impacts my brain and mood but that's super boring to me and I just don't really care. Oops, I guess that's the downside of writing a book about authentically owning your ADHD quirks.

My current favorite mellow playlist on Apple Music is called Pop Chill—current songs that are still fun to sing but with slower beats. I often listen to that while I'm cooking dinner and driving my kids to afternoon activities. It really helps lower the energy in my home and helps everyone wind down to get ready for bed. My husband loves classical music but it's just never been my thing, so I'm thankful for different options and love trying new playlists.

> **Exercise: Self-Reflection**
> - Which of these troubleshooting strategies do you want to incorporate into your life?
> - Identify one area of your life that you'd like to outsource. Text three friends to ask for a recommendation if you need one.
> - What one task do you regularly avoid that might benefit from ongoing body doubling support?
> - Find or create three playlists (focus, hype, and chill) so that you can easily pull them up as needed throughout your day.

13

Pulling It All Together

A few weeks ago, I had my best mom day ever.

In years past, I would have judged my best mom day very differently. Back then, I was much more concerned with my appearance as a good mom and having checked off all the things on my list.

But that Saturday, my feeling of accomplishment and pride was really based on how I felt.

It was an incredibly busy day. Libby's sixth birthday party was already planned for late that afternoon and then we found out that she also needed to appear in a Christmas parade that morning.

The whole family had to get out of the house by 7 a.m. and were back home at noon for some downtime before a quick turnaround to set up the party at 2:30 p.m.

As I'm also currently working on writing this book, my personal margin has been a lot lower than I'd normally prefer. Over the last several years, we've opted for very small birthday parties or skipped them all together in favor of an experience. Libby has never actually had a big birthday party and was adamant that she wanted a Taylor Swift–themed party and wanted to invite all her school, church, and neighborhood friends.

I spent weeks trying to find a place that would accommodate her vision while also keeping the planning easy and stress free for myself. I asked a local dance studio if they'd teach her and her friends a few dances to Taylor Swift songs and then kept the rest of the planning low key. I got premade cupcakes, three prepackaged snack options, water bottles, and then ordered some fake tattoos and bracelets from Amazon.

I put so much intentionality in to keeping things simple that when we found out about the parade, I was a little distraught as to whether we should participate. Her cheerleading squad was in the parade and then there was a party for all the families afterward. After consulting with Libby, we decided she'd participate in the parade but skip the party.

The morning of the parade, I ended up riding in the truck with her and her cheer friends and was able to be completely present. I wasn't distracted by the party or other priorities but felt fully myself and like I could really enjoy the event and these little girls. I had the energy to be encouraging and make them feel special.

We then grabbed a quick takeout lunch and came home for a solid two hours of downtime. I didn't rush into party prep but let the house be a mess and sat down to read a fun Christmas book.

Next, I moved into party prep mode. We kept the decorations and food simple, but it was perfect. After a lifetime of overcompensating, I had finally figured out how to create a special, simple party that was just enough. The kids had a blast, Libby felt loved, and I was fully present.

My oldest was wiped out and we chose to let him stay home to recover from a busy morning. I was able to make that decision without worrying what other moms or family members might think about his absence. I was able to confidently take everyone's needs into consideration without second-guessing myself.

I was able to help the instructor and encourage the kids who were shy or reluctant. I wasn't worried about all the little details or consumed by what people thought of everything. My sole focus was on Libby feeling loved and special and her little friends enjoying themselves.

After the party, we were all exhausted. The house was a wreck, but I let that be okay. I put on my pajamas and ordered pizza and enjoyed watching Libby play with all her new toys. That evening I climbed into bed feeling so proud of myself, not for what I accomplished or how I appeared to others, but for how I felt and how I showed up for my little girl. I had made so much progress and was truly able to focus my attention and energy on the things that matter most to me.

I couldn't have done that if I'd tried to host a big party in my home. I couldn't have done that if we'd try to also go to the cheerleading party. I couldn't have done that if I spent the downtime mindlessly scrolling. I couldn't have done that if I hadn't learned to let go of my perfectionistic ideals.

The end goal in everything that I've shared in this book is to help you climb into bed with that same feeling of contentment. I don't care how clean your home is or how many times a week you work out. This isn't about getting gold stars or proving that you are doing enough. My greatest hope for you is that *you* are proud of *you*.

> *My greatest hope for you is that you are proud of you.*

I think the hardest part of this process is letting go of our preconceived ideas for how our motherhood and family life would look. And I'll be honest, this still sneaks up on me from time to time.

> *I had visions of taking big trips as a family. Travel has yet to really work for our family.*
>
> *I had visions of being the home that hosts all the kids. My homebody kids like our home to be their personal respite and don't often like to invite friends over.*
>
> *I had visions of being an amazing homeschool mom but found that I really needed that break from my kids to be a good mom.*

New preconceived ideas that I didn't even realize I had pop up regularly. Mourning how I thought life would look versus how life looks when I accommodate the real needs of the actual people placed in my care is an ongoing thing.

If you find yourself mourning a loss, my encouragement to you is to let yourself feel that loss and disappointment and to then let it go. Only then can you move on to the important next step of creating a new vision for your family that aligns with your deepest values and makes space for everyone's needs.

The life that feels good to you—you know, that perfect mom day where you show up in a way that makes you deeply proud of yourself—will almost definitely look different from the ideal you had in your head when you first became a mom. But different isn't bad. In fact, different can be beautiful.

My challenge to you is to spend some time creating a new vision for your family that is based on this new information that you have about you, your brain, and the unique needs of your kids.

> *What does that perfect mom day look like for you?*
> *What does it feel like for your kids needs to be met?*
> *What progress do you most want to see in yourself that you can climb in bed proud of how you showed up that day?*
> *What does it look like for you to feel on top of managing your home and family life? (I don't mean that everything is perfect but that you are confident and calm knowing that you are doing enough.)*
> *What personal progress (ideas, challenges, projects) have you made as part of this transformation?*
> *When you think about this vision of your life and your family, what makes you most proud and excited about the family culture that you've created?*

Give yourself permission to create a clear vision of what you want your family life to look like that gets you deeply excited. Do this with your spouse because this isn't just about you. Throw out all the "shoulds" and preconceived ideas and get clear on what feels good to you.

You will never hear me say that learning to manage a home and family as a mom with ADHD is an easy endeavor, but man, is it good. It's a refining process that requires you to focus on what matters the most to you and let go of everything that doesn't. In the process, if you go all in, the result isn't about achieving perfection. Instead, you find the beauty of authenticity.

Letting go of the things that don't matter to you, giving yourself permission to home in on your key priorities, and owning your ADHD struggles leads to clarity and confidence. It leads to you living out of your strengths and shining despite your challenges.

> You aren't broken.
> You aren't a hot mess.
> You aren't disorganized.

> You aren't incapable of sticking to a system.
>
> You have challenges but you also have immense strengths.
>
> You do a tremendous number of boring things despite your struggles.
>
> You aren't like everyone else and that's a good thing. You were made to shine.
>
> Your creative brain brings good to the world.
>
> You are a visionary thinker and bring a unique perspective to every room that you enter.
>
> You are a gift to those who have the privilege of knowing the real you.
>
> You are uniquely qualified to raise your children and have the capacity to create a family culture that meets their unique needs.
>
> You are an amazing mom.

Know that I'm cheering you on as you do this work, but more than anything, I hope that you learn to be your own cheerleader. I hope that you begin to see the good you bring to the world, to your community, and to your family. I hope that you climb into bed this evening with eyes to see all the ways that you are showing up to take care of your brain, your home, and your family.

All My Best,

Amy

Exercise: Self-Reflection

- What does it look and feel like for your neurodivergent family to be thriving? What do you want your personal life and your family life to look like in five years?
- What do you want your personal life and your family life to look and feel like in ten years?
- What do you want your personal life and your family life to look and feel like in 25 years?

Supporting Resources

Scan this QR link to access tools and resources to help you implement the Master the Mundane system and strategies in to your life.

Sources

General Note

My strategies and insights are influenced heavily by the work of Dr. Tamara Rosier, as well as various webinars hosted by *Additude* magazine, though I don't quote these sources directly. The *Additude* magazine webinar series is available to listen wherever you listen to podcasts. And I encourage you to read Dr. Rosier's books, *Your Brain's Not Broken* and *You, Me and Our ADHD Family*, both available from Revell Publishing.

Chapter 1

National Institute of Health. (December 2024). https://www.nimh.nih.gov/health/topics/attention-deficit-hyperactivity-disorder-adhd

Arnsten, A. F. (May 1;2009). The Emerging Neurobiology of Attention Deficit Hyperactivity Disorder: The Key Role of the Prefrontal Association Cortex. *J Pediatr* 154 (5): I-S43. doi: 10.1016/j.jpeds.2009.01.018. PMID: 20596295; PMCID: PMC2894421

Kooij, J. S. (July 19, 2023). Hormonal sensitivity of mood symptoms in women with ADHD across the lifespan. *Eur Psychiatry* 66 (Suppl 1): S23. doi: 10.1192/j.eurpsy.2023.92. PMCID: PMC10417850.

Cleveland Clinic, (January 10, 2024). How Are ADHD Symptoms Different in Boys and Girls? https://health.clevelandclinic.org/adhd-symptoms-boys-vs-girls.

Shaw, P., Stringaris, A., Nigg, J., Leibenluft, E. (March2014). Emotion dysregulation in attention deficit hyperactivity disorder. *Am J Psychiatry* 171 (3): 276–93. doi: 10.1176/appi.ajp.2013.13070966. PMID: 24480998; PMCID: PMC4282137.

Katzman, M. A., Bilkey, T. S., Chokka, P. R., Fallu, A., Klassen, L. J. (August 22, 2017). Adult ADHD and comorbid disorders: clinical implications of a dimensional approach. *BMC Psychiatry* 17 (1): 302. doi: 10.1186/s12888-017-1463-3. PMID: 28830387; PMCID: PMC 5567978.

Substance Abuse and Mental Health Services Administration. DSM-5 Changes: Implications for Child Serious Emotional Disturbance [Internet]. (June 2016). Rockville (MD): Substance Abuse and Mental Health Services Administration (US); Table 7, DSM-IV to DSM-5 Attention-Deficit/Hyperactivity Disorder Comparison. https://www.ncbi.nlm.nih.gov/books/NBK519712/table/ch3.t3/.

Davis, C., Cohen, A., Davids, M., Rabindranath, A. (April 20, 2015). Attention-deficit/hyperactivity disorder in relation to addictive behaviors: a moderated-mediation analysis of personality-risk factors and sex. *Front Psychiatry* 6: 47. doi: 10.3389/fpsyt.2015.00047. PMID: 25941494; PMCID: PMC4403287.

Serine, A. D., Rosenfield, B., DiTomasso, R. A., et al. (2020). The Relationship Between Cognitive Distortions and Adult Attention-Deficit/Hyperactivity Disorder After Accounting for Comorbidities and Personality Traits. *Cogn Ther Res* 44, 967–976 doi: 10.1007/s10608-020-10115-2

Chapter 4

Barkley, R. A. (2021). *12 Principles for Raising a Child with ADHD*. Guilford Press.

Kennedy, B. (2022). *Good Inside: a Guide to Becoming the Parent You Want to Be*. Harper Wave.

Bertin, M. (2015). *Mindful Parenting for ADHD: A Guide to Cultivating Calm, Reducing Stress and Helping Children Thrive*. New Harbingers Publications.

Chapter 9

Rosenberg, S. (2017). *Accessing the Healing Power of the Vagus Nerve: Self-Help Exercises for Anxiety, Depression, Trauma and Autism*. North Atlantic Books.

Porges, S. W. (2011). *The Polyvagal Theory: Neurophysiological Foundations of Emotions, Attachment, Communication, and Self-Regulation.* W W Norton & Co.

Dana, D. (2022). *Anchored: How to Befriend Your Nervous System Using Polyvagal Theory.* Sounds True.

Chapter 12

Robbins, Mel. (July 2024). 4 Habits for Energy, Productivity, & Happiness That Changed My Life (Science-Backed). *The Mel Robbins Podcast.* 143 Studios. https://www.melrobbins.com/podcasts/episode-196.

Acknowledgments

To my incredible children, Bowman, Frank, and Libby—you are the heart of everything I do. Being your mom is my greatest privilege and accomplishment. Your maturity, authenticity, and downright amazingness inspire me to keep going every day. I'm so grateful for the way you each show up in the world.

To my husband, Mark—thank you for your unwavering support, encouragement, and kindness. You're my biggest cheerleader and advocate, and I'm beyond blessed to do life with you.

To my parents—your decision to get me diagnosed with ADD in the mid-'80s was a brave move, especially when it was far from the "cool" thing to do. Thank you for always fighting for me, advocating for me, and believing in me. Your constant support and encouragement mean more than I can say.

To my dear friends who have been cheering me on every step of the way—I'm so grateful for your excitement and encouragement, even when I've been too consumed by writing to be the friend I want to be. Your love, patience, and unwavering belief in me kept me going, and I appreciate you more than I can put into words.

To the MTM community—you've taught me so much over the years. Thank you for welcoming me into your lives, sharing your experiences, and growing alongside me. Your openness and trust have been invaluable, and I'm honored to be part of your journey.

To my Instagram followers—every like, follow, and share has meant the world to me. Your engagement and support reminded me that I have something worth sharing, and your faith in my message kept me motivated when I needed it most.

Finally, to my team at Wiley—thank you for helping me turn this dream into a reality. A special shout-out goes to my editor, Sam Ofman, for reaching out in the first place and believing I had a unique perspective to share. Your guidance, patience, and encouragement have been such a gift, especially for a first-time author. I couldn't have done this without you.

Thank you all for being part of this journey. I'm forever grateful for each and every one of you.

About the Author

Amy Marie Hann is the creator of Master the Mundane, an online course and community that empowers moms with ADHD to manage their home and family in a way that works for their brain. ADHD has touched every area of her life. She herself was diagnosed at the age of five, and her three kids, husband, dad, and sister also have ADHD. She's fostered, adopted, and homeschooled kids with ADHD and brings a wealth of personal experience, authenticity, and relatability to everything she creates. She believes that the ADHD brain is uniquely created to bring good to the world and the best thing we can do as parents of kids with ADHD is to model what it looks like to thrive with ADHD. She's a loud laugher, avid reader, and workout enthusiast with a mild obsession with dachshunds. You can find her online on Instagram at @amymariehann or at her website, www.amymariehann.com.

Index

12 Principles for Raising a Child with ADHD (Barkley), 68, 174

A

Accessing the Healing Power of the Vagus Nerve (Rosenberg), 120
Accomplishment, sense, 83
Activation zone, 25, 75
Adaptability, 14
Alarms, usage (examples), 156–157
All-or-nothing thinking, 49
Anxiety, 12
Artificial intelligence (AI), usage, 86
Attention deficit hyperactive disorder (ADHD)
 brain, truths, 33–34
 burnout, 26, 65, 81, 101, 115, 122
  depth, 168
 challenge, need, 23–26
 chronic neurological disorder, 2
 diagnosis
  absence, result, 1
  obtaining, steps, 5
 diagnostic criteria, 3–5
 fundamentals, mastery, 47, 50–51
 insights, 2–3
 intensity, 5–6
 management, 19, 35, 48, 130, 159
 misdiagnosis, 3
 severity, 5–6
 strengths, 14–15
 symptoms, 3–4
 troubleshooting, 159
 understanding, 1
 wall, hitting (appearance), 13
Automation, 139, 147
 examples, 149
Autonomy, development, 171–174

B

Back-to-back activities, 109–110
Barkley, Russell, 68, 172
Basic exercise (Rosenberg), 120
Battery, charging, 130–132, 144
 learning, 136, 142
 prioritization, 135
 time allotment, 141
Bedtime routine, 77–78
Behavior
 acknowledgment, 127
 challenges, navigation, 32, 141
Benchmarks, 139
Bertin, Mark, 68
Big black bag energy, 132, 148

Body doubling, 170–171
Boredom zone, 24–25, 106
Boring tasks, 39, 115
   child completion, expectations, 175
   handling, capacity (increase), 130
Boundaries, 36
   creation, 137
   need, 96, 176
   setting, 101–102, 112
Brain
   ADHD, impact, 106
   challenge, enjoyment, 42
   fog, 27
   function, explanation, 150
   hyperactivity, 33
Breaking it down, 162–165
Breathwork, 119
Burnout
   ADHD burnout, 26, 42, 65, 81, 101, 115, 122
   depth, 168
   exit, 116
   season, 161

C

Calendar
   electronic/monthly calendars, updating, 160
   extras, calendar example, 109
   usage, 111
   visual calendar, usage, 110–111
Capacity
   honesty, 40
   increase, 116
   limitation, 22, 177
   mapping, 151
   struggles, 32–33
Challenge
   attraction, 23
   enjoyment, 42
   increase, 74
   need, 23–26, 59–61
   pursuit, 59–60
Change
   long-term change, 48, 116
   pace, expectations, 49–50
   pursuit, 47–48
Chaos, 26, 90, 94, 137
   comfort, 107
   exit, 40–41
   life, chaos, 107
Character struggle, 106
ChatGPT, usage, 86
Children. *See* Neurodivergent children
   activities, providing, 153–154
   bedtime routine, 77
   connection, 68–69
   de-escalation, focus, 116
   downtime, need, 75
   dysregulation, assistance, 123, 126
   emotional awareness, 124
   energy, allocation, 133
   feelings, validation, 127
   moods, habits (impact), 126
   neurodivergent children, raising, 28–29, 135, 139–140
   parenting, basics, 66–67
   raising, difficulty, 28–29
   relations/emotions, navigation, 126–127
Chunking, 165–166
Clutter, impact/elimination, 89–90
Commitments
   editing, 87
   mapping, 113
   tendency, 105
Communication, improvement, 155
Connection
   defining, 68–69
   value, 76
Coping strategies, 55
Craft project, time allotment, 65
Creativity, 14, 157
Curiosity, 14, 38

D

Daily checklist, 69–71
Daily habits
  basics, 66–67
  focus, 51–52
Daily life
  appearance, 32
  chaos, 26, 40
  executive functioning skills,
    impact, 8–9
Daily rhythm, 78–80m 157
  mastery, 73
Daily stimulation, recovery (difficulty), 11
Daily three tasks
  clarity, 43
  determination, 45
  identification, 43–45
  routine, 44
Dana, Deb, 121
Days
  appearance, differences, 55–56
  low-energy days, navigation, 141–144
  mastery, 31
  normal days, appearance, 144
  planning, time (reduction), 73–74
  recovery days, 112–113
  sustainable structure, creation, 50
Decision making, difficulty, 117
Declulttering, 83, 89–90
Deep cleaning, 83, 90–91
De-escalation, 116, 123–126
Defeatism, 43
Delayed gratification, 163
Delegating, 174–178
Depletion zone, 25, 110
Diagnosis, obtaining (steps), 5
Diagnostic criteria, 3–4
Dopamine
  boost/enjoyment, 84, 106, 178
  estrogen, decrease (impact), 141
  providing, 165
Double-booking, 106
Downtime, 74–76, 154

Duvet days, 100
Dysregulated self, consideration, 118
Dysregulation, 43. *See also* Emotional dysregulation
  avoidance, 112
  perspective, 118

E

Earthing, 121
Eating, consistency, 58
Effort, praising, 82
Electronic calendar, updating, 160
Emotional dysregulation, 3, 117
  perception, 118
  repair, 126–128
Emotional regulation, 6–7, 58–59, 115
  habits, development, 116
  identification, 118
  navigation, 32
  promotion, 118–122
  struggles, 7
  understanding, 116–117
Emotional release, 54, 122–123
Emotional responses, personality (connection), 6–7
Emotions
  displays, 12
  focus, 123
  management, 47
  mastery, 115
  processing/releasing, 122
  regulation, 126–127
Empathy/compassion, 15
End goal, realization, 183
Energy, 15
  allocation, 132–133, 144
  battery, charging, 130–132, 144
  big black bag energy, 132, 148
  management, 40, 167
  mastery, 129
  mental energy, 96, 106, 135
  plan, 145
  reserving, 135

Energy (*continued*)
   tendencies, 133–141
   waste, 143
Energy-giving activities, 74
Enjoyment, embracing, 56–57
Enthusiasm, 15
Evening routine, 76–78
Executive functioning (EF), 86
   absence, results, 11
   capacity, 22–23, 33, 109
   intentional executive functioning, 34–36
   intentional plan, 143
   personal expectations, limiting, 35
   reduction, 112, 150
   requirement, 19, 48, 113, 168
   reserve, 43
   skills, impact, 8–9
Executive functions, challenges, 8–10
Exercise, 52
   basic exercise (Rosenberg), 120
   emotional release, 54
   enjoyment, 171–172
   feeling, focus, 55
   importance, 54–57
   intensity, impact, 59
   need, 28
   nonnegotiation, acceptance, 54
   vision, creation, 56
Extras
   calendar example, 109
   examples, 108
   limiting, 107–110
   mastery, 105

F
Family
   fun, 98–100
   management, 138
   neurodivergent family, care, 140
   structure/routine, creation, 65–66
   vision, 19
   weekly rhythm, 152

Fears, addressing, 161–162
Feelings
   overcompensation, 131
   validation, 127
Flow. *See* Weekly flow
Focus music, listening, 178
Forgiveness, request, 127
Foster care, 31
Friction, impact, 38
Front-loading, 167
Fun, 70, 108
   distinctions, 150
   enjoyment, 62–65
   family fun, 98–100
   increase, 74
   need, 28, 78
Fundamentals
   mastery, 47, 50–51
   sleep fundamentals, 52–54

G
Giftedness, 14
Goals
   end goal, realization, 183
   size, reduction, 165
Goals/ideas, focus, 133
Good Inside (Kennedy), 68
Grounding, 121
Guilt, feelings, 136

H
Habits
   development, 116
   focus, 51–52
   incorporation, 71, 119
   modeling, 125–126
   prioritization, 67
   regulation, 126
"Harder is easier" mindset, embracing, 166
High-energy days, 96–97
Hobbies
   fun, 63

Index

incorporation, 71
mini-hobbies, 63–64
Home project, tackling, 95
Hot tub analogy, 116–117, 124
Humor, 15
Hype music, listening, 179
Hyperactivity, masking, 13
Hyperawareness, 107
Hyperfocus, 15, 130

I

Initial daily checklist, 69–71
Insecurities, addressing, 161–162
Intentional executive functioning, 34–36
Intentionality
 absence, 108
 requirement, 41–42
Intentional parenting/learning, 140
Interest
 attraction, 23
 drive, 62
Internal dialogue, change, 135

J

Journaling, usage, 59, 75–76

K

Kennedy, Becky, 68

L

Lasting change, intentionality
 (requirement), 41–42
Life
 automation, 147
 basics, 134
 capacity, increase, 117
 change, desire, 34
 chaos, 107
 daily life, executive functioning skills
  (impact), 8–9
 daily stimulation, recovery (difficulty), 11
 design, 130
 dissecting, 162–165

management, 81–82
mastery, 31
months, mastery, 93
pace, 106
simplification, 161–162
tasks, time/energy, 18
taxing tasks, 37
transformation, 50
weeks, mastery, 81
Long-term change
 experiencing, 116
 finding, 48
Loss, mourning, 183
Low-energy days, 96–97, 141–144

M

Management issues, 173, 177–178
Masking, 12–14
Master the Mundane (MTM) system,
 36, 107, 132
 creation, 165–166
 framework, 39, 135–136, 139, 141
Meditation, 75–76
Mellow music, listening, 179
Mental challenge, outlook, 60
Mental clarity, increase, 157
Mental energy
 absence, 106, 135
 freeing, 96
 low level, 154
Mental fatigue, 10–11
Mental health, management, 2
Mental load, 108
Micromanagement, absence, 176
Mindful Parenting for ADHD (Bertin), 68
Mindset shifts, 54
Mini-hobbies
 examples, 63–64
 time, allocation, 64
Mom Admin, 83, 86–88, 177
 chronology, 88
 list, updating, 160
Money, management, 170

Monotony
  dislike, 45
  struggle, 28
Monthly calendar, updating, 160
Monthly tasks
  advice, 102–103
  identification, 95–100
  time allocation, 97
Months
  expectations, realism, 95–96
  mastery, 93
Morning routine, 74
Motherhood
  daily stimulation, recovery (difficulty), 11
  EF requirement, 19
  unique needs, 27–28
  vision, 17–18
Motherhood, ADHD
  impact, 17
  solution, 29
  struggles, 20–21
Movement
  need, masking (cessation), 55
  tendency, 105
Music, usage, 178–179

N
Needs
  communication, 126
  knowledge/ownership, 100–101
Neurodivergent children
  expectations, 174
  needs, support, 139–140
  raising, 28–29, 135, 168
Neurodivergent family, care, 140
Noise
  dread, 94
  trigger, 115
Novelty
  attraction, 23
  enjoyment, 62–65
  need, 106
Nutrition, importance, 57–58

O
Organization, perception, 151
Out-of-the-box thinking, 14
Outsourcing, 39, 167–169
Overcommitting
  cessation, actions, 106
  reasons, 106–107
Overcomplication, 41
Overeating/overdrinking, struggles, 55
Overstimulation, 10–11, 94
  avoidance, 112
  executive functioning (EF), absence (results), 11
Overwhelmed overthinker, 135–136

P
Panic attack thinking, 91
Parenting, 65–66
  ADHD majors, 66
  focus, 133
Parenting, fundamental, 50–51
Passionate procrastinator, 136–139
People-pleasing/pleaser, 12, 106
People skills, 15
Perfectionism, 12–14, 133–135
Perfectionistic ADHD, perception, 13
Perfection, pursuit (release), 145
Perseverance, 14
Personal expectations, limiting, 35
Plan, creation, 33, 137
Podcast, enjoyment, 65
Polyvagal eye roll, 119
Porges, Stephen, 119, 121
Prefrontal cortex (PFC), maturity/function, 2
Priorities, focus, 184–185
Productivity
  failure, perception, 134
  strategy, 86
Professional parent, 139–141
Progress, focus, 38
Pure Focus, listening, 178

R

Reading, time allotment, 65, 75–76, 78
Reconnection, love (usage), 127
Recovery days, 112–113
Regulated self, identification, 116
Regulating habits, modeling, 125
Regulation. *See* Emotional regulation
Rejection sensitivity, 12
Rejection sensitivity dysphoria (RSD), 12
Reminders, addition, 156
Repair, 126–127
   focus, 116
   process, 127
Risk taking, 14
Rosenberg, Stanley, 120, 121
Routines. *See* Evening routine; Weekly routine; Wind-down routines

S

Scale-based victories, 55
Schedule, overflow, 106
Screentime limits, decision, 147
Seasonal planning, 160, 166
Self-awareness/self-acceptance, importance, 28
Self-care, 70
   fundamental, 50–51
   habits, helpfulness, 51, 141
   practices, 74
   prioritization, 140
Self check-in, helpfulness, 142
Self-confidence, increase, 157
Self-discovery journey, 63
Self-esteem, low level, 12
Self-expectations, prioritization, 83
Self-improvement, 129
Services, usage, 111–112
Sleep
   adequacy, 115
   exercise habits, impact, 55
   fundamentals, 52–53
   goal, 53
   importance, 52–54
Slow and steady approach, 49–50
Social anxiety, 12, 13
Social gatherings, recovery (downtime), 28
Social settings, overeating, 13
Somatic music, types, 122
Space, creation, 117
Stimulation
   fundamental, 50–51
   need, 78
   usage, 148
Subtasks, usage, 163–165

T

Talk therapy, benefits, 122–123
Tasks
   attention, 85
   boring tasks, 39, 115
   completion, pride, 45
   list. *See* Weekly tasks.
   outsourcing, 169
   time/energy, 18
Taxing tasks, 36–38, 157
   capacity, circumstances (impact), 37
   energy allocation, 133
   focus, 133
   management, MTM system (usage), 36
Technology, usage, 155–157
Therapy
   talk therapy, usage, 122–123
   usage, 111–112
Thinking, difficulty, 117
Thought leaders, ADHD (presence), 14
Time blocking session, hosting, 171
To-do list, creation, 35, 41
Training, initiation, 172
Transformation, motivation, 173
Trauma-informed parenting, 123
Troubleshooting, 159

U

Uniquely gifted (ability), 14–15
Unproductivity, 43
Unrealistic perfectionist, 133–135
Urgency
  reliance, 26
  reserving, 137

V

Vision
  accommodation, 182
  creation, 184
Visual calendar, usage, 110–111

W

Weekly flow, 150–155, 158
Weekly rhythm (family), 152
Weekly routine, creation, 153
Weekly tasks, list, 83–84, 160
Weeks, mastery, 81
Wind-down routines, initiation, 76–77
Work
  life, changes, 138
  planning, time allotment, 164
  successfulness, 137
Working memory, ADHD (impact), 106
Work-life balance, finding, 138–139